T0381523

The Hard Times and Good Life of Bastin Lumber Company

By: Hal and Kent Bastin

Order this book online at www.trafford.com
or email orders@trafford.com

Most Trafford titles are also available at major online book retailers.

Print information available on the last page.

ISBN: 978-1-4251-4238-4 (sc)

Because of the dynamic nature of the Internet, any web addresses or links contained in this book may have changed
since publication and may no longer be valid. The views expressed in this work are solely those of the author and do
not necessarily reflect the views of the publisher, and the publisher hereby disclaims any responsibility for them.

Any people depicted in stock imagery provided by Getty Images are models,
and such images are being used for illustrative purposes only.
Certain stock imagery © Getty Images.

Trafford rev. 07/26/2018

 www.trafford.com

North America & international
toll-free: 1 888 232 4444 (USA & Canada)
fax: 812 355 4082

I would like to express my gratitude to the following persons for their help with this book:

Ben Arnold

Cecil Arnold

Alvin Brickey

Beverly Cox

Woodie Leavell

Margaret Simpson

Shelton Moss

Russell Ball

Kay Schuler

And to those who have gone on....

Cecil Sanders

Lewis Layton

Hob Bastin

Ross Bastin

Henry Clay Cox

I would like to dedicate this book to my family:

My wife Tensia, my children Kevin, Kent, Ricky and Gennie

CONTENTS

GLOSSARY OF THE BASTIN FAMILY

-Bastin, Alford. Born 01/05/1855 Died 04/10/1925

Grandfather of Hal Bastin. Started the Telephone Company and Bastin Lumber Company.

-Bastin, Allie. Born 08/21/1882 Died 01/04/1941

Wife to Alford and grandmother of Hal Bastin.

-Bastin, Bob. Born 09/16/1931 Died 02/09/2000

Brother to Hal Bastin. Ran the lumber yard for two months in 1951. Stockbroker in Louisville for thirty years.

-Bastin, Clinton. Born 09/20/1891 Died 01/20/1982

Third son of Alford, Uncle to Hal Bastin. Worked in the telephone company and ran a clothing store on Campbell Street in Lancaster from 1921 to 1924. Moved to Decauter, Georgia.

-Bastin, Hal. Born 01/06/1937

Son of Hob Bastin. Owns and manages duplexes. Managed Bastin Lumber Inc. from 1966 until present.

-Bastin, Henley. Born 04/10/1882 Died 4/11/1974

The first son of Alford Bastin. Graduated from Purdue University in electrical engineering in 1903, helped run the telephone business with his family until 1914, and also created Mint Cola in 1914. Owned the Lancaster light company in 1916-1922, Warden of the State Penitentiary in 1921-1925, Superintendent of Jefferson County Reform School (Ormsby Village) 1926-1952.

-Bastin, Hob. Born 06/12/1893 Died 10/17/1977

> Fourth son of Alford Bastin. Worked in the telephone business with family, telegraph operator in the U.S. Navy 1918. Worked at Bastin Lumber and bought business in 1921. Bought Harrison County Lumber Company in Cynthiana, Kentucky in 1924 and sold it in 1954. President of Farmers National Bank in Cynthiana. Owned Bastin Lumber Company until death in 1977.

-Bastin, Kent. Born 02/27/1983

> Son of Hal Bastin. In the U.S. Air Force 2001-2005. Student at University of Kentucky, owns and manages duplexes.

-Bastin, Kevin. Born 03/01/1980

> Son of Hal Bastin. Worked at Bastin Lumber Inc since 1998 until present. Owns and manages duplexes.

-Bastin, Ross. Born 12/13/1885 Died 11/02/1974

> Second son of Alford, Uncle to Hal Bastin, worked for the Bastin Telephone Company until 1914, owned the Lancaster light company 1916-1922. Bought Haselden Hardware Company in 1922. Mayor of Lancaster 1935-1950. Managed Bastin Lumber Company from 1943 to 1966.

-Bastin, Tensia. Born 03/11/1950

> Wife of Hal Bastin. Artist in oil paintings. Some of her works are on display at Bastin Lumber Inc.

-Goff, Bob. Born 12/0/1888 Died 12/9/1943

> Worked for Union Gas & Electric in Cincinnati, Ohio 1912-1918. Worked at Bastin Lumber 1918-1921. Bought Bastin Lumber with brother-in-law, Hob Bastin, in 1921.

-Goff, Mayme. Born 12/25/1887 Died 11/06/1978

> Only daughter of Alford Bastin. Graduated from Cincinnati Conservatory of Art 1916. Wife of Bob Goff. Some of her works are on display at Bastin Lumber Inc.

Introduction

I started on this book in the late spring of 2006 and completed it in about 10 months. It was only after the finality of this work that I actually came up with a main theme for the literary work. This book looks at the city of Lancaster through the eyes of Bastin Lumber Co. throughout the Twentieth Century.

From the move to Lancaster by Alford Bastin and his family in 1900 to the current Bastin Lumber location in 2000 the city of Lancaster is shown and revealed through the eyes of the Bastin family and, from 1912 on, through the eyes of the lumber company.

When our century started, America was a nation amongst the most powerful countries in the world. When the century ended it had become the most dominate, powerful, wealthy nation in the world. Lancaster and the Bastin family were pulled through the whirlpool of time to enjoy the progress and stress of this century.

When the century started, Lancaster was a small, back country town of about a thousand inhabitants. There were no paved roads or streets like we know today. The telephone was in its infancy. The automobile was unknown. My grandfather stated that the typewriter would be the last great invention. Perhaps it was since the modern day computer is actually based on the typewriter.

The Three S Lumber Company, operated by the Sanders Family, had the only lumber yard in the county. They did such a great job there was no need for any more. The chain yards and big boxes would not come into play for another seventy years. People would shop at home. The advertisement in the Central Record contained no phone numbers or addresses. Everyone knew where they were located so there was no need to waste space with a phone number, address or zip code. The zip code didn't come until sixty years later.

Sometimes I feel that this would have been a better time to raise a family then the end of the millennium. Then, I am so glad I learned to drive on a straight stick 1953 Ford. My brother was in the Korean conflict and had to leave a mint green '53 Ford behind. Before I totaled it on the old Russell Cave Pike about 5 miles for Lexington, I had mastered the straight gear transmission and could go from zero to sixty in fifteen seconds. My next car was a '55 Chevy Impala, Bell Air, two door hardtop. It would make the 0-60 jump in ten seconds. Fortunately, my kids never were interested in driving fast. I have asked the good Lord for forgiveness in what I must have put my parents through. I feel that I have been raised in the very best of the very best of times. Lancaster, Kentucky has had a lot to do with this good fortune I have received by living here since 1965.

My first recollection of Lancaster was when my father would have to watch over me and my brother and we would have to ride the Old US 27 from Cynthiana, Kentucky to Lancaster. About seventy miles over narrow county roads that led to a lot of motion sickness. I did not enjoy the trip at all. At the time, I did not look forward to coming to Lancaster.

I can recall walking from the lumber yard (which is my house now) down to a grocery store located where S.D. Poynter's Paint Store was located on Campbell Street. They had a big RC Cola sign on the front door. A few years later, when my brother and I had matured, we looked forward to capturing small kittens or dogs and taking them back to Cynthiana.

I can remember the new road that was created in 1952 which is the current road from Lancaster to Camp Nelson. We have a low opinion of this road now, but in 1952 when we picked up this road at the Kentucky River my car sickness disappeared. I asked my father what had happened. He only replied that we had a new road for the last twelve miles. Now, one can still see traces of the old road that went straight through Bryantsville.

Many of the stories were going on that I write about in this book on these trips, but they were far over my head....and some of them over the head of my father.

If my father knew that his youngest son would ever write about this family and bring these stories to life I would probably have been kept at home. Fathers never seem to grasp this. I was not particularly interested in his stories and everything he said seemed to go in one ear and out the other.

The reader will see that while the Bastin family never attained a lot of money, we engaged in many businesses, enterprises and undertakings. This book blends these with characters from Lancaster into this book.

I hope that the reader can see Lancaster better through the eyes of Bastin Lumber Co. and my family. I trust that the local reader will enjoy the book and that the distant reader will want to learn more about our wonderful city and its past.

Chapter 1

Deep are the Roots

Bastin is an ancient English surname and has many spellings, such as Bastian, Bastun, Bastien, Bastone, and Basden. These originate in English records back to the thirteenth century. Several genealogists from England have traced the name to a connection with a King of Wessex in 700 A.D. This is in South West England. Perhaps the name came off of the surname Sebastian which, in turn, came from the town of Sebastian in the Kingdom of Pontus. Pontus was located in Asia Minor on the coast of the Black Sea. The men of this kingdom were great travelers and seafarers. They sailed through the Straight of Gibraltar to the coast of England and traded with the English. My cousin, Charles Bastin, who now lives in England, tells me that the Bastin's came from central England in the mid seventeenth century. From there they drifted to Pennsylvania, Virginia, North Carolina, and then Kentucky.

The tax list of Caswell County, North Carolina, has the first Bastin that I can actually latch onto. His name was Thomas Bastin and he farmed and traded in furs. He was born in 1745 and died in 1817. His wife's name was Hannah and they had eight children. The eldest of these children was William B. Bastin. His father taught him to tan the hides of cattle so he could have a source of cash for trading purposes.

Thomas lived his life out along Little Wolf Island Creek which was located in the northern portion of Caswell County, right on the Virginia border.

Thomas Bastin received a land grant in 1778 and might have been one of the largest landowners in the county. The county seat is Yanceyville, which is much like Lancaster, Kentucky, as they have tobacco festivals and crafts for sale much like Garrard County. They have had murders in the town square and shoot outs in different places of business like we have had in Lancaster. Governors have hailed from that location which would remind you of our beautiful town. Too, they even have a town square.

Thomas and his family belonged to the Lick Fork Primitive Baptist Church and they are probably buried there. I am sure in a day of frontier evangelism; Thomas would be on the cutting edge. This is about all I know about my great, great grandfather. With the emergence of tobacco as a major crop in the latter part of the Eighteenth Century, slave labor became popular. Thomas and all of his ancestors after him were strongly against this practice.

Not long before Thomas died, his eldest son, William B. Bastin migrated to Pulaski County, Kentucky. The county did not have that name at the time, but that is the location where he first settled.

William B. Bastin was born in 1773 and died in 1818 when a tree that he was cutting fell on him. He took up the tanning business choosing it over farming. He especially liked Chestnut Oaks since the bark was believed to quicken the curing of cow hides. He died in Casey County and was on the 1816 tax list. He had ten children of which, my great grandfather was the second youngest.

William C. Bastin, my great grandfather was born in 1809 and moved to the Highland area of Lincoln County at an adolescent age. The first family history written by Henley V. Bastin stated that my great, great grandfather William C. Bastin was born within a few yards of the Abraham Lincoln birthplace and knew Abe well when they were children. While they were both born in 1809, the truth in this story ends. After only a little research, William C. was never close to Hodgenville. He was never close to Lincoln except in spirit.

I am sure William C. could read, write and had a good knowledge of the Bible, but he probably did not have much formal schooling. He did not favor slavery because of the way he was brought up. He did not own slaves even though he had the means too. Also, he did not lose money when the slaves were freed.

The reason he settled around Highland, in Lincoln County, was because of a large strand of Chestnut Oaks that lingered in that area. He must have been a good tanner since he was the largest in the state of Kentucky. It is said that he did business with both the North and South during the Civil War. He was located within a few miles of Hall Gap just south of Stanford.

My Uncle Henly visited the site of this tan yard in 1895 and was surprised how immense it had been. Certain parts of this operation were messy and smelly and, for these reasons, high wages were necessary. Neighbors would say, "Mr. Bastin, why don't you buy a bunch of slaves to do certain parts of this work?" His answer was always NO! He ran the yard until after the Emancipation Proclamation was signed by President Lincoln. He made and saved a small fortune. Remember, they had recessions and down economic times in those days just like we do now.

William C. Bastin's forebears were English. His wife, Mary, was born in 1812. She was a Dickerson and Irish. They both were followers of Alexander Campbell and members of the Mounty Moriah Christian Church at Highland. William became an elder in this church at an early age, and remained such for life. He and his wife are buried in the church's grave yard close by.

Two of William's sons, Alexander and Martin, served in the Union Army during the Civil War. They were mustered in and out of that army at Camp Dick Robinson.

My grandfather, Alford H. Bastin, was born January 10, 1855, and again, was the second youngest in the family. He did not like to work in the tanning yards, but was afraid to rebel. This trait of family business, togetherness would stay with the Bastin's down through our generations. Perhaps the hard work helped to shape his character.

He studied pedagogy at Transylvania from 1872 to 1874. This two year period was ample time, in those days, to entitle him to a teaching position. Today, this would be a major in education. He taught eight years in Crab Orchard, Kentucky.

My other great grandfather was Martin Ross. His forbears came to America from Ross County, Scotland. He became a slave-owner and depended on them since he had little family help on his large farm in Lincoln County. Martin was a strong Baptist and thought he could justify slavery by the English Bible.

Martin was born in 1817 and married Malinda McClure in 1848. She was born in 1830, was Irish, and approved of his slavery beliefs. He lost his slaves after the Civil War, but was able to buy back a forty acre portion of his original farm. It was about a mile from Crab Orchard. He and his wife and three daughters lived there.

The oldest daughter, Catherine, born in 1862, married Thomas Dulaney, of Illinois, a Republican and a Northerner. This disturbed Martin because of his beliefs. He warned the other two girls not to do this. They both listened.

My grandmother, Allie Ross, daughter of Martin, was born in 1858, and became a teacher after graduating from Tarrants Academy, June 1875. She taught at Crab Orchard, Kentucky.

At this point it might be well to review the social situation of this troubled town, which was torn between three factions that despised each other. While all three factions spoke English, they were not on speaking terms with each other. Shootings and killings occurred often and Crab Orchard became a dangerous place to live.

Crab Orchard had not less than six different kinds of mineral water within a radius of two miles of its center, or Crab Orchard Springs. These wells were under the control of the Springs Hotel Company. This hotel had a capacity of about five hundred adults, plus children and nurses. The water was filled with sulfur and many felt a conviction that it had medicinal properties.

For forty years the Springs Hotel was filled to capacity for most of the year. These were people with northern sentiments from northern states, and they remained aloof from local residents who were about equally divided between the north and the south in their sentiments.

Like Caesar's Gaul, Crab Orchard was divided into these three parts, and each was severed from the others. The war was over, but the feelings were as bitter as ever.

The town people finally decided that the war was over and they would bury the hatchet, but not very deep. At this time Alford had completed his education in Lexington and had been teaching a couple of years at Crab Orchard. Here, he met his future bride, Allie Ross. Now, Dan Cupid started to work.

Alford Bastin, my grandfather of the North met Allie Ross, of the South; both started a teaching profession. A spark of mutual interest was lighted and soon it burned brightly. Feelings of guilt made contacts rare and infrequent. Finally, love found a way and won. Alford proposed and Allie accepted on the condition that they wait until she became twenty-one and legally free.

Both taught school in different locations in town. While Alford didn't think he could wait, Allie stuck to her convictions and would not marry until she was twenty-one.

Alford did not know her father, Martin Ross, except by sight and feared greatly to meet him. By looking at his picture, I would too! However, there was no getting around the meeting. Allie lived with her parents and rode a horse to and from school each day. Meetings had become difficult.

When Allie was almost twenty-one, Alford said to her, "I am going to ask Mr. Ross now. I cannot wait any longer." Allie replied, "I fear the storm you will raise. Please wait until Sunday and it might go down easier."

Sunday came and so did Alford. He rode his horse, General Grant and he arrived on time and hitched his horse to the yard gate and went to the house to find Mr. Ross waiting on the porch. Martin knew what he was going to ask. "What do you want, boy?" asked Mr. Ross. Alford replied, "I would like to marry your daughter, Allie."

Mr. Ross barked out, "Are you a Baptist?" Alford replied, "No, I am a member of the Christian Church." "Are you a Democrat?" Mr. Ross demanded. "No, I am a Republican," Alford answered. The last question that Martin asked was Alford's views about freeing the slaves. Alford said that he was in favor of the emancipation of the slaves. "You are wrong on every point," said Mr. Ross. Now get on your way and don't come back. The door was slammed in his face and Alford beat a path.

On August 21, 1879 Allie became free, in her sight, and she met Alford at the home of Rev. Jasper Livingston, the minister of the local Christian Church, and they were swiftly wedded.

The bride and groom rode away on a brief honeymoon and the preacher rode over to the home of Mr. and Mrs. Ross to break the news to them. "Are they legally married?" asked Mr. Ross. "Yes", the preacher replied. Martin asked the preacher to sit on the porch while he and his wife, Melinda talked it over inside. After about ten minutes, the couple returned with tears in their eyes and asked the preacher to pray for them. Martin wanted to do the right thing and would ask God to give them the wisdom to act in a way pleasing to him. Too, he asked the preacher to give him the understanding and grace to accept this new son in law. After a prayer, he said "Amen."

Then, Mr. Ross told the preacher to go and tell them to come to their home after the honeymoon and live with them and share their home. Tell them that we have enough canned food in the pantry for all to eat. We have enough wood to keep our fires burning to keep us warm and to cook our food. We have enough love in our hearts to care for them and their horses without cost. We want them to be free in order to be good teachers, because education can help our broken nation. My grandfather and his new bride came to live with his in laws for eleven years, until the death of Mr. Ross in 1890. Mrs. Ross sold the farm and made her home with the Bastin's until her death in 1899. I have pictures of this family, including, Mrs. Ross, on the front porch of their home in 1894.

Alford taught school for eight years until 1882. Allie taught only one more year after marriage, or until 1882. In 1882 the couple had their first child, Henley. He would be the only one to graduate from college. All of their children did well, but perhaps Henley stood out in his professional career. Ross Bastin, who was best known in Lancaster, was born next in 1885, Mayme, the only daughter, in 1887, Clinton in 1890 and Hob, my father, in 1893. All except Hob and Clinton are buried in the Lancaster Cemetery.

Alford bought a small saw mill and general store in partnership with J. Harvey Collier and operated under the name of Bastin and Collier. This business started in 1882. My family has been in the lumber business actually since 1882.

In 1890, Bastin and Collier split up so Bastin could build a new store along the railroad track in Crab Orchard. This store sold everything the customer needed and would buy all of the produce that the customer might want to sell. He operated on a cash basis at this time on the theory that such a plan was best for the customer and the merchant.

Times got complex and money was tight so Alford broke the rule. He issued his own money in denominations of one, five, ten, twenty five cents and a dollar. This was readily accepted for all country produce.

This included split and hewed lumber such as boards for roofing, spokes for wagons, ties for railroads, staves for barrels. Strict records were kept for all of the Bastin's money issued. With good credit money for the purchase of goods from wholesalers was readily borrowed from the National Bank in Stanford.

From all of the evidence that I can gather in writing this book, I can say that my grandfather, Alford Bastin was a man of great integrity and honor. He stayed in this business until January 1, 1900, at which time he sold it and moved to Lancaster to buy the local telephone exchange. His mother in law had passed away and he had the means to get into another business.

There is a possibility of something happening that I am not really sure of. He did not like people owing him money and not paying when they should. However, it seemed to bother Alford more than the normal run of the mill businessman. Lenord Boone, a cousin and a former county judge of Lincoln County told me that Alford might have killed someone over business problems.

James Bastin, Alford Bastin 1906

Hob Bastin, Clinton Bastin
In front of the Citizens' National Bank - 1900

Martin and Melinda Ross- Alford's in-laws 1856

The Bastin family 1888
L to R Henley, Alford, Ross, Allie, Mayme

Chapter 2

The Telephone Business

On the first day of the New Year, January of 1900, Alford Bastin packed up his family of six: a wife, one daughter, and four boys and moved to Lancaster. On one of the moving trips, my Dad, Hob, told me that as a seven year old, he remembered seeing the gas lights of Lancaster from a distance. The highway connecting the two small towns was only a dirt road and, at this time, had serviced only horses and buggies. Remember, it would be nothing like what we have today.

Alford had purchased the house that I live in today from Smith Wortham, who had inherited it from his father, Hiram Wortham. Alford bought it for nine hundred dollars. The Central Record stated that Alford would make many repairs to this house. At this time, the house came all the way out to Campbell Street. In 1954, my Dad would cut twelve feet off the front of the house to make a nice front yard for his sister, Mayme, who would live here until she died in 1978. Actually, the house lost about four hundred and eighty square feet in this remodeling effort.

In the back yard, there existed a small shed that would make way for a large barn in 1914 where lumber would be stored, and parts of that barn still exist today. As soon as Alford was set in his new home, he went about one of his most important enterprises, the telephone company. In about 1896, Dr. Kinnard got permission from the City Council to have a phone line installed from his home to his office. Immediately, other lines were installed and an exchange created. While it was not much, there were about one hundred phones in existence in the town when my grandfather took it over in 1900.

His first exchange was located over what is now the Subway restaurant on the Public Square. This would be in the south west portion of the square. At that time Storms Drug Store was located there. Grandfather was quick to improve services and equipment. His eldest son, Henley, was now eighteen years old, going on fifty. He helped install the complicated equipment while on spring and summer break from Purdue University. He would later graduate from Purdue in 1903 with a degree in electrical engineering. Henley, Hob, Ross, and Clinton would prove to be excellent, discounted help. Henley declined offers from several large companies in Chicago to come back to Kentucky and work for his family. This trait, as we have mentioned before, has stayed with the Bastin family until this day.

At this time, Lancaster had a population of about one thousand four hundred sixty, while Stanford had one thousand six hundred fifty-one and Richmond had four thousand six hundred fifty-five. The local roads were not in good shape and it would be twenty years before they would be rocked, tarred and passable. Alford had his work cut out for him.

The Central Record, which I will refer to as the Record, stated that this family put their whole soul in the service that they gave with the phone company. "No town has better service than Lancaster," stated the Record in late January of 1901. "All calls are answered promptly and the instruments work well." Too, it said that ".....no monkey business is permitted and it is hard to see how we got along without a telephone before."

In early 1901, the Record gave Mr. Bastin's advice on how to use a telephone. The lips should be one inch away form the speaker. You were instructed to have a mental focus on what you planned to say. You should be prompt with your business since other people might need to use the line. The operator was depending on you to enunciate your request clearly. You were encouraged to be courteous. Do not ask the operator about the weather or his/her personal life, and do your business quick.

At first, the Bastin Telephone Company did not manage long distance calls. They were made from McRoberts Drug Store. This was located where Danny Irvin has his real estate office now on the public square. A few years later, they were moved to the Garrard Hotel.

The Bastin's got into this business in its infancy. They made improvements, ran new and improved lines in the county, secured outside contracts, and now, by 1902, had given this small town an excellent exchange. Alford installed first class lines, and replaced small crooked poles with straight ones. He made sure he hired excellent operators to support the growing business. At this time, the Bell System offered him and excellent deal, but he refused. At the time, Alford was on top of the world.

Although the Bell System had a monopoly on phones, there were many independents operating in America. Alford Bastin had one of these in Lancaster. At first, the Bell System chose to compete with the independents in the courts rather than trying to provide better and cheaper service. When law suits began to favor the independents, Bell finally gave up the legal attack and made an effort to improve service and lower costs. This is the reason that the City Council would not allow Bell into Lancaster. The county would not trust them.

Western Electric, the equipment supplier to Bell, would not sell to the independents like the Bastin's; he had to buy from a company in Chicago, named Monarch. Too, he sometimes bought from The Electric Telephone Company of Kokomo, Indiana. As you might imagine, the independent companies were mainly rural in the South and Midwest. At this time, 1900, the independents had more customers than Bell.

In March, 1900 the Bastin Telephone Company put on drive to increase subscriptions. The Bastin's offered to donate all of the net profits that month to a fund that would support the purchase of two iron gates for the cemetery. I feel sure that this helped obtain the gates on Crab Orchard Street to some extent.

On June 14, 1900 Mr. Bastin was elected vice-president of an association of area towns to co-ordinate telephone service in Central Kentucky. The cities that met were Cynthiana, Winchester, Lexington, and

Knoxville, Tennessee. The telephone lines would go between a metallic circuit to connect Cincinnati and Knoxville. By this time, 1900, all local towns in Central Kentucky were connected.

On November 8, 1900 the Central Record praised the Bastin Telephone Company for the rapid manner in which they reported the election. The Record stated that "We have one of the best exchanges in the state!" It was true; Alford and his boys put long hours into this enterprise. He had connected Lancaster with every important part of the state.

On July 4, 1901 Alford Bastin advertised in the Record stating that if as many as ten were going to Crab Orchard Springs for supper, he would call Mr. Willis, the manager, to make reservations. Of course for Alford, there was no charge for the call.

In 1901 there were seventy independent telephone companies in Kentucky with around fifteen thousand phones. Bell offered to allow the independents to use its new line from Lexington to Newport. Eventually, it would make it easier for people in Lancaster to call other states.

On September 2, 1901, the Bastin Phone Company purchased a new switchboard. It was the best money could buy, as it had four hundred drops as well as the latest improvements. The bell rings when the receiver is taken off, as this did away with the old crank system. It will also ring off when one is through talking and hangs up the receiver. With the new switchboard it will be much more convenient. Bastin stated that "I am not going to stop until Lancaster has the best telephone system in Kentucky."

In late November of 1901, the Record states that the City Council turned down a bid by the Bell System to set up a rival exchange in Lancaster. This type of protection helped not only Lancaster, but my family. If Bell had a local franchise, rates would have gone up and service would have turned for the worse once my family sold the business or went broke. The Bell System at the time was arrogant and extremely aggressive when they had a monopoly in a town.

Lower rates and the appeal of the underdog made the independents popular and usually able to win the referendums that could decided who might control a town's phone calls. Like every other business, competition would result in better service and lower rates. Bastin's rates remained at one dollar per month for residences and one dollar fifty cents for a business. As long as Bastin would give great service, the City Council would protect them.

In large cities like Boston there might be three or four telephone companies, and Bell would certainly be one of them. In cities where this occurred, there was a tendency for sides to be drawn along class lines. The competing systems would not be interconnected, so it was only possible to talk only to those on your system. If you wanted to talk to your friends, you would have to be on their system. To talk to everyone, you had to have three or four phones in your house. Seldom did anyone have this. The rich class usually had the expensive Bell System. Perhaps the middle class made up of professional workers would have another system and so on. Thus the telephone became a sort of electric class maker that might be described in the old Boston jingle went about like this:

The land of the bean and the cod,

Where the Lowell's speak only to the Cabots

And the Cabots speak only to God.

Many areas had situations where independent farmers or do-it-yourself, non-profit telephone systems developed. A group of farmers who lived close to each other would meet together and arrange to establish a telephone system which would connect them with one another. The farmers would each contribute material and labor to the mutual task. The wire and the insulators, the switchboard and the instruments, would have to be bought. The work of stringing the wires and installing instruments was taken up by the mechanically minded farmers and their boys. With this cooperation, soon a complete telephone system was in operation. The switchboard was placed in the home of one of the members of the association situated at a convenient point and lines attended to by a wife or daughters of that home.

The twentieth century decline in the art of letter writing, which can legitimately be laid at the telephone's door, is only one symptom of the manner of communications. The fact seems only to be that the United States is the telephone's natural home and the twentieth its natural century. The instruments and people found each other when the century just started. Alford Bastin was caught up in this movement of culture mixed with technology.

Alford and the telephone brought a new hero to the local public …the rural operator. In the natural course of things, she became an involuntary message center. The locals would say, "Oh, Central! Ring me up in twenty minutes, so I will remember to turn the stove off." Or, perhaps they might say, "Central, call me in one hour so I won't miss the train." Central became a heroine, intelligent, level headed and self sacrificing, solving problem adviser that worked for free.

Remember, these days were pre-radio. The telephone brought the farmer news and companionship. The newspapers at first feared this incursion into their domain, but the reverse proved to be true. The appetite for communications grows by what it feeds on. Many people today watch only the news shows such as the Fox News Network or Cable News Network (CNN). Back in the early 1900's, you had to search for the news.

In the rural areas party lines were the rule rather than the exception. Often, eavesdropping on the neighbors came to be a standard entertainment, sometimes producing quarrels. Often, it took rudeness to obtain the phone for an emergency call.

One of the funny stories that Alford passed on to me through my father concerned a rural customer of his in about 1904. The subscriber took the transmitter apart to see what made it work. In doing so, he spilled the granular carbon. Being unable to retrieve the carbon, he decided that it looked pretty much like gunpowder. He installed this substitute as he put it back together and then manipulated the switch hook. Bang! Just picture the damage. My dad did not share the final results with me.

America, as well as Garrard County, was becoming a slave to the telephone. Like the television years later, its effect on life in general was widespread. The increase in the number of rural phones between 1902 and 1907 was phenomenal-from two hundred seventy thousand to one million five hundred thousand. Too, the states with the densest concentrations of telephones per population were the states such as Iowa, Nebraska, California, and Nevada, not the Eastern, big city states.

The Bastin family was fortunate to have Henley, age 19, blessed with the intelligence to do the technical jobs. Ross, Hob and Clinton would do the more basic jobs. Alford would manage the whole affair. My father did not like this operation; one reason was because he had to be night operator many times. This interfered with his lessons in school as well as his social life. He was about eight years old and vowed to have his own business someday. He wanted to be his own boss. In time, this would come true.

In 1903, Bastin started to use the Kellogg Switchboard & Supply Company for their needs in Lancaster. Since they seemed to be in competition with Western Electric, Bastin thought that he was buying from someone who was not owned by the Bell System. He was wrong! It came out that they were controlled by agents of his competition that had been pledged to secrecy. It started to dawn on Alford Bastin that this would be a difficult, competitive business to be in.

The local editor liked my grandfather a lot. He played jokes on Alford and Jim Hamilton in many editions of his paper. His name was Luther Landrum and I was very impressed with his editorial work as I paged through the early issues of the Record in the Twentieth Century. One story that he made up told of the havoc on the telephone exchange, located over Storms Drug Store, in 1901. Landrum said that Alford Bastin was eating his lunch at his desk when a bomb went off down in the drug store. Alford was lifted up, as if by magic, all the way to the ceiling. When this large man hit the floor, bottles and merchandise in the store below crashed to the floor. The clerks in the drug store ran as fast as possible into the street thinking that the building had fallen. Dr. Kinnard was called and checked the flow of cuss words that came from Alford. No one was hurt, except Mr. Bastin's feelings.

Many stories like this one were reported about my grandfather. None, I am sure, were true. One could see, however, that Mr. Landrum liked those whom he joked about. Too, the exposure was not bad for my family business.

Another story in the record went like this. Granddad met Jim Hamilton on the square. Alford said to Jim, "Jim, I will bet you five dollars that you cannot recite the Lord's Prayer." Mr. Hamilton took him up on his bet. He started out, "Now I lay me down to sleep, I pray the Lord my soul to keep, if I should die before I wake...." "All right," declared Mr. Bastin, "I did not know you knew so much about the Bible. Here is your five dollars."

While it is an amusing story, I am sure that it, like the bomb in the Storm's Drug Store, did not happen. My grandfather would not make such a bet feeling that it might be sacrilegious. Too, he would know that Mr. Hamilton would have been wrong. Alford knew the Bible well enough to know that was not the Lord's Prayer. It did prove that Luther Landrum liked both Jim Hamilton and my grandfather.

The Record would help the Bastin Telephone Company by telling the public that the operators could not make twenty calls at once. Be patient! Don't be unreasonable. The local office is the best managed exchange in Central Kentucky and should be treated with respect. A gentleman or a lady will display good manners.

Were there Problems? Yes, the exchange had them in the early part of the Twentieth Century. Some boys from Somerset cut the lines going to Danville along Hubble Road. In those days, the telephone lines ran from Lancaster to Hubble and there to Hedgeville and then to Danville. Lancaster was not able to call Danville for several days since those boys severed the lines. The boys were caught and sent to jail, but the Bastin's had to, at their expense, repair the lines. This is what my Dad dreaded.

In 1903, the Record stated that Alford took the local exchange when only a few lines were in use and turned it into one of the most efficient in the state. His subscribers will attest to this. Also, the paper boasted on Henley with his degree in electrical engineering from Purdue. It mentions that Henley got a lot of practice at West Lafayette, Indiana. At this time, Alford's eldest son was twenty-one years old. We will follow his colorful career as we go along in this book. He is what held the phone company together from a technical point.

In 1903 the Bastin family moved into the Governor Bradley House or House of Seven Gables on Lexington Street. Alford rented the house from Governor Bradley. Only a few years ago, Pete Glich bought this house, tore it down and built a beautiful ranch house in its place. I was happy since I got the materials on the new house. However, many in Lancaster who were interested in history being preserved did not like the idea. There is just not enough money to buy all of the places of historic interest and preserve them.

By December of 1903 the independent companies had forty-five thousand customers in Kentucky while the Bell System had twenty-three thousand. You can see that Bell was not really interested in the rural states.

Another utility was about to be born in Lancaster. On August 7, 1903 the City Council released the contract of the local water works. The cost was twenty-four thousand four hundred forty-one dollars and the

Bradford Company out of Louisville purchased it. This meant at least thirty years of debt since pipes, engines, forty-five fire plugs, a reservoir close to the south end of town of ten acres had to be purchased. The pipes would be eight inches in diameter on the main streets and six inches in diameter on side streets. Two engines would furnish the pressure and both would operate during the day, but only one at night.

In January of 1905, the Bastin Telephone Company would receive locust or cedar posts in lots of twenty-five to two hundred. They would be delivered between Clayton Arnold's and Bryantsville on the Lexington Pike. The Bastin Company would install new lines from Bryantsville to Buena Vista.

By 1906, the local exchange had so many new numbers that it now asked the customer to give the number you are calling. The operator cannot memorize all of the new numbers. The Record asks the people to "Learn how to use your phone."

In February of 1907, the Record stated that Bastin is putting out a new telephone directory. "If you want your name in it, act now! Do not wait. Call up the exchange and give your name and spell it distinctly for the operator." On this same month, Bastin installed a phone at Dripping Springs, so the famous resort would have communications.

On July 19, 1907 the Bastin Telephone Company moved from the second floor of the Storms Drug Store (now Subway) to the second floor of the Garrard Bank Building (Whitaker Bank). At this time, there were five hundred wires to change around, so the town could expect some patience. Perhaps there would be a twenty-four hour period where there would be no service. Henley Bastin had graduated from Purdue and worked full time at the exchange. The Record stated that Bastin gave the best service in the state. While I am proud of this accomplishment of my forbearers, I realize that Luther Landrum might have exaggerated some in his praise of the phone company.

Later in that same month, he pointed out that Lancaster had the lowest rates in the entire state. This must have been true since Lancaster people would complain and ask rates to be lowered if it were not. The town people did not realize that this telephone company was being subsidized by cheap, first-class, family labor. This would come back in a few years to haunt the town, city council and the phone company.

By March 6, 1908 Lancaster has a new hotel, the Kingarland. The town needed it to house traveling salesmen, family visitors, and travelers. This hotel was located next door to the telephone exchange, which is now a parking lot for the Whitaker Bank. My Father, Hob, was about fifteen years old and was a happy camper. He told me that since there was no decent hotel in town, guests would stay at their home. He would have to get up early and bake biscuits for breakfast and help in the kitchen. He hated for family guests to drop in for this reason. Now they could be put up at the nice hotel which made life easier on Hob. When I was a child, I remember my Dad would always ask Mom if it was all right to have guests over to spend the night. She usually agreed, but it did not happen much.

One of the most prominent business men in town was injured by our home on 201 South Campbell Street about this time. Banks Hudson, one of the largest dealers in hemp, coal, and seed was visiting our home. When he was passing the depot his horse was frightened by the hissing sound of the steam engine of the train. The horse hit Mr. Hudson's buggy and drug him about twenty feet. He was rushed to his residence on Danville Street where Dr. Kinnard looked at him. The doctor put a cast on his chin that made it difficult to talk or eat. It took several months for this outstanding entrepreneur to recover and take walks down Danville Street as he always loved to do. His grain elevator was located on South Campbell Street just a block south of where Bastin Lumber Inc is located today. If one looks at the Sanborn Insurance map of the town in 1915, they could see how impressive Banks Hudson's business was.

During the tenure of Alford Bastin's ownership of the Bastin Telephone Company from 1900 to 1914, there were three editors of the Central Record. The first, Luther Landrum, ran the paper from the second floor of the Citizens Bank Building. He was the most favorable to our phone company. Sometimes his articles on the company seemed like flattery. You can imagine how this helped the infant company get a jump start in a utility that would soon become competitive and then, eventually, unable to compete with large companies such as the Bell System.

Green Clay Walker was the second editor during the tenure of Alford Bastin's time in the telephone business. He liked my grandfather, but mentioned him only a few times in the paper where Luther mentioned him almost every week. Too, while Mr. Walker said nothing but good things about the phone company, it was not as often. Also, there were not as many references made about Alford's family.

Green Clay Walker only managed the paper for about four years. He improved the coverage of minorities in the community. It seemed like he gave African-Americans more respect. Then, when Joe Robinson took over the paper, there was little mention of the Bastin Telephone Company. This was around 1914. The First World War was about to start so Editor Robinson gave that crisis a lot of attention, and he did this rightfully so.

In 1914, the courts decided that the county could control the phone lines and electric lines that ran along side of the roads. The cities already had that power. This gave the county the same degree of control as the city. The city would have the power to give anyone they wanted the right to the telephone lines. If the phone company would raise rates, the city could give a competitive company the franchise. If the city council would favor the Bastin Telephone Company, if and when they would raise rates, the people of the county would complain.

Bastin kept rates down for two reasons. Both reasons were pushed thin by current events and would make it impossible for any telephone company to keep the rates the same. First, Bastin employed his family at almost serf labor. They worked as a family, but the boys had little to show for it. But no one else could do this. Mr. Bastin always had a large house and would let his female operator's room and board with the family. This way, he was out very little except for material expenses. The materials did not go up much from 1900 to 1914 and in some cases of overproduction, went down. As long as both factors were in play, Bastin could keep everyone happy. In business, it is impossible to keep everyone content. Alford evidently saw the First World War coming. My Dad told me that he was uncanny about sensing when business might make an up turn or a great change. In any case, Alford thought that the time to sale the phone company was 1913.

In 1912, the Record mentioned that the City Council decided to allow the best deal to take over the phone company. If Bastin offered it fine. If not, go with another phone company that would promise to keep rates low. While Alford did not like this, he saw the handwriting on the wall. Since the editor of the paper had changed and the council had new members, Alford wanted to get out of the business as soon as possible.

While he had printed new telephone books every few years, he stopped this practice. Instead, he would list about ten or so new numbers in the Record and tell people to cut this list out of the newspaper and glue it into their old book. He was out to save money anyway possible. He knew that he could not raise his rates or there would be problems. They had to stay one dollar per month for residences and one dollar fifty cents for a business.

By 1912, Clinton Bastin left the family business to take a position with the Houstonville exchange. Clinton, age twenty-one, would be a big loss to the family business. Only a few days after Clinton left, the Titanic went down in the freezing Atlantic Ocean. The Record stated that it was lost over two miles under water. The Record did an excellent job of reporting on world events.

In the spring of 1912, Bastin installed forty-seven new numbers. Some were Dr. William Elliott #220, Dr. B. C. Rose #379, and the Lancaster Tobacco Warehouse#186. Again, Alford asked people to cut this from the paper and glue it into their phone books. Later that year, Henley Bastin, the chief electrician, caught malaria fever. This about did the Bastin family in. Henley could still tell the other boys what to do, but he could work little for the next year. This was another nail in the coffin of our telephone business.

The Bastin's did get break when the Hubble Exchange ran their lines to ours over Old Danville Road. Even with this extra business, Bastin did not dare raise rates. He knew that the city and county would not permit it. He knew the time to sell is now.

The Cumberland Telephone Company of Somerset had taken over several small towns like Lancaster. They were pushing to get Bastin out and bring themselves in. They promised the stars, and the moon. The City

Council listened, but by a close vote, stayed with our family's business. At this time in the telephone business, the larger you were the greater the cost. The council seemed to grasp this and, for the time being, stayed with the Bastin exchange.

By 1913, the real dynamo of the business, Henley was well and ready to start his own business. He had witnessed the creation of Coca Cola in Atlanta and actually visited that city to see how this miracle soft drink was manufactured. He felt that he could do the same in Lancaster. Henley and the Haselden family went together and created Mint Cola. Some fortunate people in the county still have an actual bottle of this local cola that might have made it to the top like Coke. John S. Haselden was the other partner in this venture. In February of 1914, it was manufactured at the home of M. T. West on Lexington Street. You do not hear much about this new Lancaster product after 1914.

The paper did say something interesting though about Henley and Clinton. It said that "these two young men got their start at the Bastin Telephone Company and made the very best of this circumstance. They were fortunate and made good and look where they are now. They have made it." While both were good citizens, both would have many rocky roads to go over before calling it quits in the business area of their lives. It is dangerous and perhaps bad luck to ever say you "have it made." The Record actually stated they were on "Easy Street!"

Henley left the phone company for a week or so to go to

Chattanooga, Tennessee to a conference on the possibility of a highway going from the city of Cincinnati, Ohio. It would go right through Lancaster. This was more important than the mundane work in a local telephone exchange. This was the last straw for my Grandfather. He now had only my father, Hob, to work the lines and sub for night work at the switchboard. This had to be the time to sell.

No one had the money in cash to pay what Alford wanted. Mr. J. R. Cornn approached my Grandfather about the phone company. While he had little cash, he owned a lot of rough lumber in many dimensions that he would trade for the phone company. I do not know how much lumber was offered in this trade, but it must have been a lot. I recall my Dad telling me that he put his overalls on and helped unload and stack the lumber. I made the mistake of asking my Dad if he actually handled this large amount of lumber. I had only seen him in a business suit, never in work clothes. His answer would not print in this book.

In any case, by 1913 we were out of the telephone business and into the lumber business. The lumber was delivered to a lot where the old Cowden Factory is now located on Hamilton Avenue. We stayed there only one year and moved to Campbell Street, where we have been since 1914.

While the United States did not enter the First World War until 1917, we were a major supplier of materials, wire, steel, food and many other commodities to the European nations at war. This caused mass inflation. All materials to run an exchange on went up, up, up. Mr. Cornn never had a chance.

Mr. Cornn went before the City Council and asked for a raise in rates. He wanted to go to a modest one dollar and fifty cents a month for residences from the one dollar that Alford had charged. A business rate would go from one dollar fifty cents to two dollars. While this seems fare to us now, this represented a fifty percent raise. The Council did not have a chance to decide since a general meeting was called at the court house to protest. My uncle, Ross Bastin was the only one at the overflow meeting to take up for the new managers. While Alford did not get the cash he wanted, he at least got out by the skin of his teeth. Like it or not, our family had to learn the lumber business and take a shot at it.

Now, Joe Robinson, the editor of the Record, would not back the local phone company. The Bastin family did not own it any longer and an outsider was now managing the company. Still, it carried the Bastin Telephone Company name up through most of the 1920's.

Mr. Cornn said, and rightfully so, that when the one dollar per month rate was established, land sold for forty dollars and acre. Now, in 1916, it was selling for up to one hundred forty dollars an acre. Telephone wire had gone up three hundred percent. Mr. Bastin had spoiled the town in using his family until even they left for better jobs. He could not do these things. The First World War was causing major inflation and he could not stay in business unless rates were raised and quick. In April of

1916, the City Council went to the contract that Bastin had signed sixteen years ago and demanded that it be met. By March 7, 1918 Mattie Lutz is the new manager of Bastin Telephone Company and Charlie Moore is the chief lineman. Daylight saving time is now introduced to Garrard County and the Central Record has just printed a thirty-six page telephone directory. Luther Landrum, the good friend and editor of the Record, has just passed away in Danville to make 1918 an unusual year for the Bastin Telephone Company.

In May of 1919, the phone company got a jolt when it was announced that they would not get a rate increase. On June 5, 1919, it was auctioned off on the courthouse steps. Ironically, the folks that now owned the Bastin Telephone Company were the only ones to bid on it. This proved that when Alford Bastin accepted a large bunch of rough lumber in trade for his 1913 telephone company, it was not such a bad deal. Because of the stinginess of the City Council and, ultimately, the customers of the local phone company, it held little value. Alford saw this coming. He had moved out just in time.

You can see the many factors that played a part in the demise of this infant company. The inflation of the First World War, the loss of support from the Central Record when Luther Landrum sold out, the breakup of the pool of cheap family labor and the failure of the City Council to award an appropriate rate increase led to the failure of the phone company.

Now, since the same people that owned the phone company bid it in on the courthouse steps, a rate increase was granted larger than Mr. Cornn had originally asked for. Rates were pegged at one dollar sixty-five cents for a residence and two dollars fifty cents a month for a business. Look at what it took for justice to be met. Again, Alford Bastin seemed almost uncanny in knowing when to bail out of this interesting venture. When our family sold the company we had about one hundred ninety phones in the city and five hundred in the county. Figure it out. There was no profit for the phone company.

The telephone was so important that in 1918 when Lenin took over Moscow and the Kremlin, he had to find a nice residence that was hooked up with a telephone. He took over a villa about twenty-five miles south of that ancient fortress that was once owned by the writer, Maxim Gorky.

My wife and I visited this site, which proved to be one of the finest colonial homes that I ever stepped into. I have traveled through Mississippi and Louisiana and been impressed with their anti-bellum architecture and colonial homes. None of this would compare with this opulent mansion. I saw little of sacrifice that the Communist claim is a necessity in his style of life after he came to power. He was a first class hypocrite since this residence had a telephone and he could get in touch with Stalin at the Kremlin at a distance of twenty-five miles. The phone was in place before the Revolution; since it took several years after the blood shed was over for even the most mundane of necessities could be obtained during the Revolution. Even in Russia, the phone was a big deal.

No Garrard County Farm
Residence is Complete
Without a

Telephone

It is no longer a luxury, but a necessity.

It facilitates transportation, commerce and industry.

It develops neigborliness not only among, but between communities.

Don't impose upon your neighbor when a Telephone can be enstalled in your own home for a moderate sum.

We stand ready to serve you at any time.

BASTIN TELEPHONE CO.

LANCASTER,   KENTUCKY.

One of the first Bastin Telephone advertisements

Banks Hudson
Lancaster business man
1914

Chapter 3

Luther Herron, the Police Chief

Police officers are a strange breed. Some are driven by being zealous, some by a passion for the truth, some by a sense of justice. Some are naive about the traditions of our democracy and American way of life. Some are on a personal mission to clean up the world. Some enjoy the power of a uniform. Some are motivated by the desire to be revered as an authority figure. A few are honest men dedicating their career to public service. Which of the above Luther Herron was is up to the beholder. Perhaps he was a mixture of all.

In 1905, the City Council of Lancaster was desperate. Desperate times demand a desperate decision. Policeman, George Pollard had been shot in cold blood by a white bootlegger by the name of William Hubble. The shooting was over a local option law that was broken by Hubble. At the time, there was much unrest in Lancaster about the buying and selling of liquor and beer. The editor of the Central Record, Luther Landrum, said that Hubble was one of the wets and for the murder of officer Pollard he should hang. Later, on November 2, 1906, Hubble got a light sentence for the day and deed. He received a life sentence. Usually, this type of crime might mean public hanging on the square.

The Chief of Police was S. D. Rothwell at the time of the murder of Officer Pollard. While being an honest policeman, an Andy Griffith type, he was not suited for a town with the potential for violence that Lancaster was in 1905. The City Council did not have far to look. The trial of Luther Herron in Harrodsburg had just been completed. He had shot a legislator, Sam Black, in what some called a dual.

SHOOT OUT AT THE COLEMAN'S STABLE

The story of the dual killing started out on a hot, steamy night in August of 1905 at Coleman's Livery Stable in the Rosser Building in Harrodsburg. Luther Herron and another officer, William Britton, were planning to raid a saloon run by Walter Stotts. The two officers thought that Mr. Stotts ran gambling rooms upstairs over his saloon. Britton went into the saloon and accused Scotts of these illegal activities and had loud words. Officer Britton then went next door to the livery stable and planned the arrest with Luther Herron.

They talked over the serious charges against Mr. Stotts and brought up the fact that Stotts, some months ago, had broken up an arrest of a bootlegger they almost caught. It seemed that the police officers were later charged with holding a grudge against Walter Stotts because of his actions.

These operations were called Blind Tiger operations. Harrodsburg was like all small Kentucky towns. It was plagued with gambling and shooting craps, when it was illegal in that town. Herron and Britton were disgusted when one of their schemes failed. As we follow the career of Luther Herron it will become crystal clear that he did not like failure. He was a work-a-holic who paid little attention to salary or payment for services. He always attended to whatever business was at hand.

While the two officers were planning the arrest, Walter Stotts came running out of his saloon shouting and cursing the two police officers. A young man, Walter Vincent, from Jessamine County was passing by at this time and he testified that he heard Stotts curse the officers and ask if they planned to arrest him. At this time, Britton rose up and said to Herron, "Let's arrest him." Stotts jumped at Britton and grabbed the officer's pistol. Just behind Stotts was his legislator, Sam Black of Harrodsburg. Mr. Black was thirty-eight years old and a member of the legislature from Mercer County. Too, he was a prominent educator who had been friends with Stotts and represented him in several cases in the past. One can only feel sorry for this legislator who seemed to be at the wrong place at the wrong time.

At this time, the county superintendent of schools, Floyd Taylor, entered the fray and placed his arms around both officer Britton and Black and urged peace. It was at that moment that the first shot was fired. Mr. Taylor was burned in the face by the powder of the shot and could not tell who actually fired the shot. Then he fled for his life. It was the two officers against Black and Stotts. Apparently Luther Herron had shot Sam Black and then turned his pistol on Walter Stotts, and in a matter of seconds, had killed them both. In the confusion, either Black or Stotts had shot Officer Britton in the face. It looked like three or four men in the dual were dead.

Policeman Britton walked across the street on his on strength, and seated himself in a chair in front of the newspaper (Harrodsburg Herald) office and remarked, "they have killed me too." It turned out that he had been shot by either Black or Stotts in the head. This wound turned out to be serious, but not deadly.

Later, at the inquest, Luther Herron stated that when he pulled Stotts into the stable, he jerked loose from him and fired the first shot, which hit Officer Britton. Officer Britton stated that he hand no alternative but to defend himself and his fellow officer.

The scene looked like the O K Corral with Wyatt Earp and Doc Holiday. There were at least fourteen shots fired. Stotts emptied out his six-shooter. Britton had fired five times and Luther Herron had fired three times. As usual, Luther Herron did the most damage with the least shots fired.

Joe Freeman, who witnessed the shooting, says the first shot came from inside the stable. Since Luther Herron was the only one in that location, it must have been him, if Freeman was correct. This shot killed Mr. Black. Superintendent Floyd Taylor agreed with this version. He was the one who had a hand on Burton and Black. He stated that the bullet passed so close to him that it felt that someone had tossed sand in his face.

For some reason, Joe Freeman ran through the saloon of Stotts with a pistol waving it in his hand. He told people to keep their seats and not to become involved with this tragedy.

A man named Clarence Tower was the first witness to reach the dying saloon keeper, Stotts. When the fusillade of fire ceased, Tower found Stotts on his knees. He asked Stotts to give him his pistol and the wounded man handed it over to him with the remark, "Take it. I have done all I can do."

Mr. Stotts friends all unite in saying he was sober and left his saloon in good spirits. They also state that he ran no gambling house over the saloon and he had never been notified that he must close a gambling house over his saloon.

The wonder is that more people had not been struck by bullets, since there were fourteen shots fired. Sam Black's pistol was lying by his side unfired. Two were dead and one may be dying. This is the resume of the career of the man who the City of Lancaster would hire as policeman and later, town marshal and/or police chief.

At the coroner's inquest it was found that Sam Black was shot twice, once in the head, going through and breaking his neck and the other passing through his body. He died instantly. Stotts was shot clear through his body at the right breast and died minutes after the shoot out. Officer Britton was shot in the head and recovered. Luther Herron was not wounded at all. This good fortune would not remain with Luther Herron for the rest of his career.

If the Lancaster Council would be faulted with little research, an examination of the records in Mercer County would prove different. Luther Herron had a well deserved reputation of getting the job done. In January of 1904, he caught Arthur Parr stealing chickens and chased him down. Mr. Parr was fined ten dollars and cost, and worst of all, consigned to the work house. All of these small towns needed the jails to be full since this is where the labor came to clean the city streets. The streets needed oiled and rocked at least once a year. If there was no one in jail, the city had to hire workers. This was difficult with such a low tax base.

In May of 1904, Luther was called to look into some reckless shooting. It appeared that some Danville men had taken a horse in a surrey and shot up Harrodsburg. After this spree, they had retreated back to Danville. By shrewd detective work, they learned about five Danville men had taken the rig and gone to Harrodsburg. One of the five had turned states evidence and revealed his companions. They were fined seventeen dollars each and cost. The informer was fined one dollar. This was excellent work. Officer Herron would produce work like this in Lancaster in the years to come.

The next item on Luther's record occurred on September 11, 1904. Luther had arrested eight laborers on the railroad east of town for disorderly conduct in the rear of the Turf Exchange Saloon. This was at a time Harrodsburg was wet. Of the eight, only Bill Jones put up a fight and broke away and ran. Herron gave pursuit and fired one shot as a warning to make Jones stop. He did not heed the warning shot, but Luther overtook him on Depot Street. A terrific struggle took place while Jones tried to wrestle the pistol from Herron. Herron realized he was losing his strength and shot Jones. This would be a signature of Luther's throughout his career. No one would escape. No matter what the circumstances were. I feel that it was his idea of doing a complete job rather than being cruel. Jones later died that night because there was no one to tend to his wounds. It seemed that Luther had to help out with more arrests and for this reason could not help Jones.

Luther Herron was always tried in a court of law after he killed someone. He always gave his pistol up after the fight was over and never resisted arrest. He believed in law and order. Every jury always returned a verdict of acquittal. Too, this jury would exonerate Mr. Herron in a short time.

While there were other cases that would point out the abilities of this unusual policeman in his short Harrodsburg tenure, the city fathers of Lancaster had a good idea of who they were hiring.

Luther Herron was born in Willisburg in Washington County in 1870. The Civil War had not been over but five years and this was an era of violence in Kentucky. He was raised on a farm with brothers and sisters. While a youth he moved to Cornishville in Mercer County. He was known as a fearless lad while growing up near Harrodsburg. As far as we know, he played no sports in school. In fact, he had little formal schooling. He could read and write and do math well enough to get most any civil job of the day. He later would turn into an excellent business man.

In fact, the first document that I examined concerning Luther Herron was his contract signed on January 1, 1904 to work as a policeman for the City of Harrodsburg. He had a stately signature and excellent hand writing. As far as we know, he killed at least seven people in that city before resigning and coming to Lancaster.

On May 4, 1906, Luther was hired to work on the police force as a regular patrolman for the City of Lancaster. This was a trial period even though the council was sure that this was their man for future police chief. James Beazley was the chief at this time since S. D. Rothwell had stepped down from that office. Luther Landrum, the editor of the Central Record, said that Herron was a fearless officer and that is just what the town needed. On the May 7, 1906 issue of the Central Record it showed a picture of the slain police officer, George Pollard. He had a wife and three children in the picture with him, who was now without a husband and father.

On May 14, 1906 the Central Record stated that Mr. Herron had been hired to root out all of the town drunks and evil. There is no mistake about it; Luther Herron was hired to combat excessive alcohol abuse. This was only a month after George Pollard was shot. On November 2, 1906 William Hubble got a life sentence for shooting the police officer. I find this hard to believe, since many of the people of Lancaster wanted to hang him right on the square.

Luther was a diplomatic type of policeman. He did many things one would not expect of a man of this office. In January of 1907, he entertained the city council with a goose supper. The meal was served by a Mrs. Zimmerman.

His first test came when William Hubble and Jones Simpson broke out of the local jail. They sawed the bars on the window and escaped before inspection time on April 9, 1907. This was not long before Mr. Hubble was to be sent to Frankfort to the state penitentiary. Simpson had been sent to jail for twenty-one years for burning a house with people still inside. Hubble's sentence was life. The paper stated that Luther was on their track as soon as the jailer discovered them missing. By April 26, 1907, Hubble had been caught by Herron and not long after Simpson turned up in the Madison County Jail. It might be interesting to note that James I. Hamilton worked for the defense in the Hubble case.

By December 20, 1907 the town of Lancaster seemed to fall in love with this strict law enforcement officer. Luther Landrum, editor of the Central Record stated that both blacks and whites liked him. Now, Chief Beazley is going to retire and the council wants Luther Herron to take over as police chief or town marshal. Sometimes he is referred to with both titles. The paper states that Luther has stamped out the Blind Tigers (local bootleggers).

On January 3, 1908, Mrs. George Pollard, wife of the officer that was shot in 1906, died after a short illness. She and her husband left six children at their small home on Danville Street. The town, out of sympathy for these orphans, raised quite a sum of money. The leading contributor was none other than James I. Hamilton. My grandfather, Alfred Bastin, was generous as well. Lancaster seemed like a nice place to live and raise a family in spite of all of the shootings and local option problems.

In February 1908, John Romis, a fugitive from Tennessee who had killed several people was now on the prowl. He had been spotted working for the L & N Railroad as a section hand somewhere in Garrard County. Even though this occurred outside of the city limits, Luther moved on a tip and captured the criminal and collected a reward. Again, Luther seems to have no fear of anyone when making an arrest. He was a born policeman.

On March 8, 1908 he was instructed to enforce the vagrant law. Anyone who does not have visible means of support will be taken to the court house and tried and if found guilty, sentenced to hard labor. The town had to pay for repairing the streets if no one was in jail to do this work. The Central Record took the position that no one should be left to be an idle loafer, no matter how well they dressed, you went to jail if you had no visible means of support. One can see that this would get the bootleggers who dressed well, but could not show how they obtained the money. The stores would accept the money for the nice clothes, but after this the city would throw them in jail.

By 1911, Luther had enforced the 'local option' law that said you could not give, furnish, lend, sell, and provide any liquor product. A fine of fifty to one hundred dollars and ten days in jail would be given out if you were caught for any of these offenses.

About this time, Luther lost one of his best friends, Jacob Joseph, a Jewish man, who had been born in Germany and immigrated to Lancaster in 1880. Luther would hang around Mr. Joseph's store located on the southeast corner of the square where the First Southern Community Center is now located. Lancaster was lucky to have its local Jewish store as did many Central Kentucky towns. In Cynthiana, where I was born and raised, it was the Pressmans. This family like the Joseph's gave of their means to the poor. Both families were staked to a business by relatives and friends of their race. Both families took advantage of their good fortune in life and gave back to society much more than they were given. Through hard work and saving, excellent manners and spiritual resources, these families help provide a backbone to the American way of life. Luther Herron knew this and mourned with the passing of Jacob Joseph. Jacob was buried in a Jewish Cemetery in Cincinnati located in Walnut Hills. He is not to be confused with Simon Joseph who died in 1957. He was a native of Turkey and a peddler in the Bryantsville area. He was buried in the Lancaster cemetery.

Think of the fate that these two families would have suffered if they remained in their native lands. Hitler killed all of the Jews in Prussia where Mr. Joseph hailed from, and German SS murdered most of the Jews in the Ukraine where the Cynthiana Pressman's came from. Joe Pressman was able to slip out of Czarist Ukraine in 1914. As soon as he landed in America, he was mustered in the army and had to fight in France two years later. He returned to make a wonderful success in business and raised a splendid family in Cynthiana. I was friends with some of his children. In fact one of them was a noted actor in The Winds of War and had his own sit com in the 1970's.

Luther Herron would have been lucky if all the citizens of Lancaster were like the Josephs. As the reader will see later, it was not to be. Still, he not only was and excellent policeman, but encouraged his family to mix and integrate with the locals. His son Sammy and my father were acquaintances. In fact, much of what I know about Luther Herron came from stories my Dad told me on the way to see the Cincinnati Reds play in the late 1940's and early 1950's. We would talk baseball on the way to the game from Cynthiana on US 27, but on the way back we would talk Lancaster history. Luther Herron and Jim Hamilton were two of the things we talked about. I can remember them more than anything else.

Luther did it all. He had to cope with the new invention, the automobile. How fast should one drive in the city? Who would determine what the speed limit was to be? Luther Herron! Too, Luther managed and collected bills for the water department. A good friend of mine remembered Luther well. Jake Marsee gave me an accurate picture with words of what Mr. Herron looked like. Jake described him as stocky, with a full mustache and a western cowboy hat. When I actually found a picture of this police officer, I could identify him by the description that Mr. Marsee gave me. Cecil Sanders told me that Luther lived on Stanford Street near the Christian Church. At first this was hard to believe since this area is all business now. However, when I looked at a Sanborn Map that was created by engineers I found that Cecil was correct. At that time, in 1915, you had the Rex Theater where the Garrard Hardware Store is now, Luther Herron's house, and then Romans Carriage Shop. In fact, Luther Herron built the main portion of Garrard Hardware with designer block to be used as a garage in the basement, a theater on the first floor and a dance hall on the top floor. He lived next door in a house that was demolished in the 1960's and was a neighbor to Romans Carriage Shop. If one would examine the Central Record from 1900 to 1925; you would find that Mr. Romans would have about as many advertisements as Joseph's dry goods store.

Luther was good with the streets of Lancaster. He noticed that adjoining towns would oil the gravel at least once a year, perhaps in May, to eliminate dust. He made sure that this was done in Lancaster. In 1912 the old school, called Lancaster School, was torn down to make room for the new, modern Lancaster Grade School. A contractor by the name of

O.P. Raymond from Cynthiana got the job. While Mr. Raymond was a man of principal, he brought workers with him that the Chief of Police had to keep an eye on. At some point, the fear of the Almighty was instilled in this bunch of carpenters.

Most interesting, Luther kept the Sabbath and its laws. Perhaps out of respect for Mr. Joseph or the church crowd. He made sure that baseball and fun games would not be played in public on Sunday. Even though Sunday is not the actual Sabbath, I can remember back in Cynthiana that many frowned on playing on that day like it was any other day of the week. On November 8, 1912 Judge E.W. Harris enforced these laws and made children stay home. Perhaps this was going a little far. Please keep in mind, Luther was enforcing the laws that were on the books. Each year Lancaster had a county fair. Luther made sure that the Blind Tigers did not sell their wares at this public event.

As I wandered through the Central Record for information on this colorful man, I wondered how much the city had to pay him. Perhaps he enjoyed the authority and work so much, he might work for free. I am sure the council would have liked that. However, he got four hundred twenty dollars a month for being town marshal and one hundred eighty dollars for being the Superintendent of the water works. He collected all of the bills for the city water. Believe me, this was a job. Can you imagine collecting from the lowest ten percent of the cities customers?

In 1911, Stanford had a crook by the name of George McRoberts who was slick with checks. He was hard to catch since he would go from town to town and then stay low for a short while. As in all cases, sooner or later the crook will make a mistake. George's was to come to Lancaster to try this forgery. Luther took all Central Kentucky newspapers and remembered what he had read. He happened to see a strange man plodding through the snow in a heavy fur coat. After investigation, he checked with a local bank and found that it was his man wanted in Stanford. Luther was always eager to cooperate with sister towns. He would expect to get the same cooperation from them. Luther had no trouble with the arrest of McRoberts.

In 1913, Luther and lovely wife, Margaret, bought the property that is now Garrard Hardware. They purchased it from China and L.B. Conn. Her name really was China! Then Luther proceeded to build a theater on the main floor with a garage in the basement. The third floor would be a dance hall. The building would be constructed out of decorative block and would be a beautiful addition to the city. Until I did the research on this project, I did not have the faintest idea of a theater being at this location much less a dance hall. I cannot imagine anyone doing a history of Lancaster or Garrard County without including this most colorful character and his family.

Luther was interested in the sidewalks of the town as well as the streets. On January 31, 1914 he asked the residents of Water Street (Maple Avenue) to complete the wood sidewalks in front of their homes so pedestrians could walk by without getting in the mud. Because of the immense amount of grading it would be difficult to put concrete in for sidewalks.

On April 4, 1914 Luther filed charges against the L & N Railway for violating the Webb Act. It seems that the L & N delivered several barrels of beer to a local option county. The town marshal said that the county will abide by the Webb Act, which prohibits the selling of spirits.

Those of us who like old western movies can recall how cattle and livestock would be run through a town and how the dust would fly. Well, Lancaster was no different. The Chief put a stop to this in 1914. He told farmers to handle their livestock in a responsible manner or face a large fine.

The Central Record states that Luther worked night and day. In the August 15, 1914 edition said that a night policeman is now needed. Since Luther Herron cannot stay up night and day. Think of it! This man tends to all police work, the water department, city sidewalks and streets as well as collecting taxes. The man seems to be worked to death.

It is August of 1914 and the First World War starts with the assignation of Archduke in Sarajevo. While the United States stays out of the fray for two more years, there is a spirit to join the service among young people. Sammy Herron, the eldest son of Luther decides to do this. Sammy was an excellent student in high school as well as an outstanding baseball pitcher. The reason that I know this is because my father, Hob Bastin, was his catcher. In an April 1909 issue of the Central Record it was stated that Sammy Herron and Hob Bastin, the Lancaster battery struck out ten Nicholasville batters. In those days, the battery, both pitcher and catcher were given credit for strike outs. Not just the pitcher. My Dad said that Luther's children were raised with good manners and respect. They were all tough like their father, but were a credit to their parents as history would soon prove.

On September 19, 1914, Sammy enlisted in the Navy in Columbus, Ohio. He promised to be home for Christmas, since this was not yet war time. This enlistment would land Sammy in the Philippine Islands for the next several years and keep him out of dangerous combat in France. He had two brothers who would not fair so well.

One of the more violent crimes took place in 1914 that faced Luther's tenure as Chief in

Lancaster. It seems that he had jurisdiction in the county as well as the city. On Mt. Hebron Road, at the home of Thomas Doolin, a certain Richard Spivy, age twenty-three, stabbed Bryan Dyehouse, age eighteen with a pocket knife. Luther had to come all the way from Lancaster to arrest Spivy. There was seldom resistance when this officer came to do his job. He took Spivy to jail on a two thousand dollar bond that could not be made. It was found that they were drinking Tiger whiskey when the event happened. This galvanized Luther's opinion against this evil even more. It will lead to an event in his life that one can hardly believe.

The Strange Case of Robert Strange

Late on the hot, sultry afternoon of June 14, 1914 Luther was summoned to the home of a Ms. Jayne Burton. The paper said that there was a fight between John Gibbs and John Strunk. When Luther arrived the fight was not so difficult to break up by itself. It seems that there was another man there under the influence of alcohol. This man had no business butting into the fray, but did for whatever reason. The reason might never be known, but perhaps because he disliked authority. Maybe he did not like Chief Herron getting by with an easy afternoon. But why did he interfere? After the story is told, you too will wonder. Trouble could have been nipped in the bud!

No sooner had the Chief straightened the problems of Gibbs and Strunk, a newcomer to town started arguing with him. No one seems to know exactly where Robert Strange came from or why he needlessly provoked this officer from leaving the scene of trouble. Luther did not like to be challenged and this he was. After being told to get out of the way, words came to push and shove. At this time the Chief attempted to place Robert under arrest. Robert took off running and, Luther chased him. He finally caught him by the stable of W. R. Ball.

At this point of the arrest, Robert turned and tried to wrestle the gun from Luther's hand. Sounds like the Bill Jones case in Harrodsburg several years earlier. Jones tried to wrestle the gun from Luther's hand and was shot. Luther did not want this to happen again. While he was a fearless lawman, he did not like shooting people.

Robert finally got the pistol and shot Luther in the side of the head above his eyes and through the brain! That's right, through the brain and above the eyes. This seems impossible and the paper states that it was impossible. Miraculous! Amazing! Then, on top of that, another shot hit him in the left chest, and another three shots went wild. My father was in town that day and recalled the scene, the blood and even brains soiled the street! I realize that this is difficult to believe but this is the way bystanders described what happened. With something like this happening, I cannot understand why there has not been more written about this piece of history in Lancaster.

The Central Record stated that now Robert Strange went straight to jail on his own. Since Luther had no backup or deputy, Robert could have escaped. This is what you would have expected. But no! He went straight to the historic jail of Garrard County. All the time he was waving the unloaded gun threatening anyone who got in his way. "All stepped aside." He said that if he had more bullets he would have put them into Luther's body and made sure of his act.

The Record said that the bullet went below the brain and above the optic nerve. This resulted in a bad headache and the loss of sight for a day or so.

Robert was locked up in the jail while Luther was taken to his home with a doctor in attendance. The June 18, 1914 issue of the Central

Record said that Luther Herron was doing nicely and was expected to make a complete recovery! He had lost his sight for a day or so, but this expected to improve, and it did! He was back on his job in three weeks.

Nothing could be done with Robert Strange until Luther either got well or died. Since it was apparent that Robert had killed no one, he was sentenced to several years in the penitentiary at Frankfort. Several years later, my Uncle Henly V. Bastin would be the Superintendent of this institution. It seems that Mr. Strange was given a six year term for his needless actions. This is another strange part of the whole affair. One would think that in that day and time, perhaps a hanging would be in order. To the credit of Lancaster, this did not come close to happening. Throughout the tenure of this police chief or marshal, one will find that no one was railroaded, and Civil rights would be held to a high standard. Perhaps it was the watchful eye of Joe Robinson, the editor of the Central Record.

On August 14, 1914, only two months after being shot in the head Luther welcomed Harry Faulkner to Lancaster. He had just made a seven hundred mile auto trip from Philadelphia. He had few mishaps which included several flat tires. He, as all drivers in those days, was equipped to fix them. Some states did not oil the roads and blacktop as we know today, then it was almost nonexistent. People today just do not realize the conditions of the roads and poor directions of that time.

He now had to establish the speed limits in Lancaster. I have no record of Luther ever driving a car. He probably did since the paper indicated that he went for a ride with his wife just after the shooting. Perhaps it was a buggy ride! I do not know for sure.

Frank and Briss Conn had a garage just behind Luther's theater, which was named the Rex. Luther's two sons ran the projector and generally managed the business. Frank, who had been financed by James I. Hamilton, sold Buick automobiles. Frank was always after Luther to buy a big, black Buick. Luther was very conservative with his money and was not ready to go into the auto age. Later, Luther would sell this desirable property to several investors. It was about this time, July 1914 that the first Coca Cola ad showed up in the Central Record.

On November 19, 1914 the First World War was at a stalemate on the Western Front and Chief Herron opened his theater on the grounds of the now standing Garrard Hardware. The main floor will seat four hundred and a suspended balcony would add another hundred.

In the spring of 1915, Luther Herron resigned as town marshal. People were surprised at this action since law enforcement was all that he knew. Lee Prewitt was named acting marshal until one could be named. By late April, Orville Buck from Junction City was named Police Chief. He had broken up a bootlegger bunch in that town several months ago. Orville seemed well qualified for the job, but did not have the notches in his pistol that Luther had.

Another Strange Happening

On April 29, 1915 Robert Strange almost escaped from the penitentiary. This man, who really should not have been locked up in the first place, planned to engineer his own fate again. He bent the bars on his cell window to where he felt that he could slip between them. Still, he had a sixty foot drop. By tying his bed clothing together, he could negotiate at least forty feet of this drop. After dropping the line made of sheets and blankets, he got stuck in the small window. He could not move in or out. He was stuck! He was a determined man. If he would go to this extreme to escape there must be a bigger motive than freedom. His independence would be given in about three or four years on good conduct.

As I examine this strange case, I am reminded of the Gary Cooper movie High Noon. This was a popular cult type movie of the early nineteen fifties. Gary Cooper as sheriff sends Old Tom Creech to prison. While in prison Tom makes a vow to kill Cooper or die trying. The lyrics went like this:

Old Tom Creech made a vow while in state prison,

Vowed it'd be my life or hisn,

Oh, darling, what will I do?

His darling was acted by Grace Kelly. I do not know if Mrs. Margaret Herron would fit in this puzzle as Grace Kelly or not. But one can see the resemblance of High Noon. Follow the narrative and you will see the setting for another great movie starring Luther Herron with Lancaster, Kentucky as a replacement for a western town.

Robert shows how bad he wants to get at Luther by making this almost impossible attempt to escape. After reading this history in the Central Record, I do not believe anything is impossible. Nothing! Only because Robert could not extricate himself from the window he did not break out of prison. It will be three more years before he could enact this fantasy.

If Luther has any worry about Robert breaking out of jail there is no mention of it in the paper or gossip by the town folks. In 1916, my father, Hob Bastin, was working as a clerk for his Dad in the newly formed Bastin Lumber Company. While we started on Hamilton Avenue in 1913, by 1916 we had moved next to the depot on Campbell Street where we are located now. My father never mentioned Robert's attempted break from prison.

By January of 1916, the city council was between a rock and a hard place. Half of the council wanted Orville Buck and the other half wanted Luther back as marshal. Luther had become a legend by this time. He would be hard to replace. Mayor Davidson will have to break the tie. He does by voting for Orville. Luther does not seem to mind since he helps make arrests from time to time. He still commanded respect.

On June 15, 1916, Luther is appointed game warden. This man just loves authority. The paper states that he will enforce the fish and wild life laws and will prosecute anyone who breaks them. It is difficult to do this job and run the theater at the same time. One of the other will have to give.

At the end of the summer of 1916 he sells the Rex Theater to Walter Hammock. His sons do not like this idea since it puts them out of work. Still, the theater sells for eight thousand dollars.

By October of 1916, Luther is back as city Marshal. Mr. Buck does not like this and objects. Too, Orville did not like the idea of separating the job of Marshal and Superintendent of water works. He did not like to lose the salary base which paid an additional sixty dollars a month. However, by November of 1917, Luther resigns a second time. W. S. Carrier is elected Chief of Police and Luther seems to pursue other interests.

In late 1917, Luther's middle son, Story Herron, got in a fight with the son of the County Judge. It seems that Story and Forrest Stepp had their eye on the same Lancaster girl. After Luther's son whipped him, a fine of fifty dollars was levied. Luther did not protest. In all of the actions of the Herron's from 1905 until they moved out of town in the late twenties, this is the only bad mark against the family.

By 1917, the Herron's had three boys in the service. In 1918 Stanley was wounded at the front in France in heavy combat. Risking his own life, he aided several comrades and was recommended for medals. His brother, Sterling, was wounded in a battle zone near Chateau Theriry. He was taken to a Red Cross hospital in England with wounds that were not life threatening. The third son, Sammy, was stationed in the Philippines and did not see the action that his brothers experienced. Of all of the Herron children, Sammy might have been most suited for combat.

In March of 1918 James I. Hamilton buys the Rex Garage. Jim is no more modern than Luther, but likes to be on the cutting edge of business. He feels that the automobile is here to stay. Jim rents the garage to others for nine hundred dollars a year.

In January 1919, Teddy Roosevelt died on his estate on Oyster Bay in New York. Luther has lost his commander in the Spanish American War. If there was one person that Luther looked up to it was Teddy Roosevelt. He was a veteran of the Spanish-American War under Teddy Roosevelt in Cuba. Luther was too old for the First World War since he was forty-four at the start of the conflict.

Since Luther is Superintendent of the water works, he enforces the rule that everyone must have a water meter. This will be the only way the city could measure how much each person uses rather than just charge a standard fee to all. The meters will cost fifteen dollars each.

At this time, the summer of 1919, Luther's neighbor, W. S. Romans, is having a hardware sale. The Romans Buggy Works was located on Stanford Street next to Luther's house. It is the exact spot where Cecil Arnold built his insurance office and now is the law office of Johnny Bolton. The Record says that the sale included lawn mowers, ice cream freezers, coal oil stoves, and many other items. Luther's sons, who all have a first name that starts with the letter S, are in the Romans Theater located on Richmond Street where the Stump's Grocery Store was located. They actually rented this building from Mr. Romans.

Nearing High Noon

In the 1950 movie High Noon, Gary Cooper is the town sheriff that is awaiting the arrival on the noon train of a criminal that has been released from prison. The criminal arrives as expected and the movie centers on a gunfight that Cooper, the sheriff, wins. What now happens in the life of Luther Herron comes close to this movie.

Robert Strange is now released from the state prison in Frankfort. My Uncle, Henley Bastin, warned Robert not to come back to Lancaster since Luther would get him. Later, Henley will be made warden of this state penitentiary. Really, the trouble started years ago when Robert butted into an arrest that he had no business being involved in.

Now it is May 20, 1920 and Lancaster has become a stage on which an apocalyptic final battle will be fought between law and order and rebellion. This is a drama that seemed destined to happen. Perhaps its outcome was decided by fate. It should never have happened.

While Robert Strange had been released from prison before the terrible day arrived, he came back to Lancaster on the eleven a.m. train: not the noon train in the movie. My father was a clerk at his Dad's lumber yard next to the depot. He thought that the gun fight took place as soon as

Robert got off of the train. The depositions of the case prove somewhat different.

Saufley Hughes (1877-1971), saw Robert go from the depot to the town square and circle around toward Danville Street close to Storms Drug Store. The Subway Restaurant is located there now. Mr. Hughes was talking to Chief Herron closer to the court house. Strange would keep looking in a threatening way at the Chief of Police. Herron continued on toward the Police court room which is the Court Annex now.

Mr. Hughes stated that he was surprised to see the men so close together considering the trouble they had years ago. The way Robert stared at Luther attracted Mr. Hughes attention even more.

Hughes went on to state that Robert had walked at a fast pace all the way on a direct line from Joseph's Dry Goods Store (First Southern Community room now) toward Storms Drug Store. During this time, Luther walked at a normal pace toward the Police Court room.

This is the end of the deposition in behalf of the defendant. No other record exists except the account in the Central Record and Kentucky Advocate. The accounts jive with my father's testimony from this point on.

It seems that Luther went from the Police court room toward the depot with Strange following him. As they passed Bastin Lumber Company on Campbell Street and just before the depot, Luther Herron all of a sudden unloaded on the aggressor with three shots in his left side. It is believed that two of the shots passed through his heart. Robert Strange died instantly. The killing happened at eleven o'clock that morning. It is ironic that if we were on daylight savings time, it would have been exactly high noon! The Danville paper added that "Luther Herron, who has a number of notches on his pistol, adds another today."

In only three more years, another dual would shock Lancaster and Garrard County much the same manner this event unfolded. James I. Hamilton, on this beautiful day in May, has a countdown of 1,129 more days to live the colorful life of a country gentleman. We will come to that later.

On March 23, 1921 Luther Herron was acquitted by a jury in circuit court. We failed to mention that Luther, as usual, gave his gun up and turned himself in without even being asked. He had no doubt of his acquittal. The announcement of the verdict was followed by an outburst of applause in the crowed court room.

While my father did not witness the actual shooting, he was close by. From what he knew, it was a fair fight. He only wondered why Robert started the fracas in the first place. Too, he wondered just why Robert would come back to Lancaster. My father liked Luther's children and played baseball with them. My Dad had little time to socialize since he had to help with the phone company. He was lucky even to get to play baseball. The best I remember, he thought Chief Herron was a strict, but honorable man.

While Luther was waiting for the results of the Grand Jury, several events happened to his family that brought the realities of life home. His son, Story, who most people nicknamed "Slick" married a very nice young lady. While only seventeen, she complained of massive pains in her side, which ended up in a trip to the hospital. On February 17, 1921 she died of a bad case of appendicitis in the Danville Hospital. The funeral was held at Luther's home on Stanford Street.

The only other time I recall of this young man being mentioned was in the context of his habit of challenging anyone who might come along to wrestle or fight. He hung around at the tavern run by Tiny Merida, close to where McDonald's is located today. Too, Slick had a habit of following carnivals and circuses around to challenge their strong men to a wrestling match. He generally won these matches.

In April of 1921, Luther was deputized and helped arrest William George and William Leasure on the charge of moon shining. Tom Ballard was a deputy sheriff at this time.

Stanley Herron, the son that Lancaster would remember most, married Miss Gladys Frisbie. Stanley worked at the pool room and worked the soft drink stand of Herron and Cox. Sammy, home from a stint in the Navy, took a job with Black Mountain Coal Company in Harlin County. Later, he was promoted to deputy sheriff. The paper said that all were confident that he would do a good job.

Two years later, Sammy married a Miss Elizabeth Middelton in

Cincinnati. The paper said that they will live in Corbin where he will take a good job with the L & N Railway as a policeman. Most of the boys were drawn into police work.

By 1925, Luther had another career with the new Dix River Dam as security man. He apparently arrested someone who had connections since he landed in jail himself. The charges were carrying a concealed weapon. It seems that he could carry a hand gun on Garrard County side of the dam, but could not on the Mercer County side. Perhaps the Mercer County sheriff remembered him from 1904. In any case, it took a pardon from Governor Fields to release Luther.

By 1930, Luther Herron was a citizen of Boyle County. The main events of his life have passed and he would spend the balance of his seven years in relative peace. He lived on West Broadway close to where the public library is located today. He took his last job as a security guard for the Farmers Bank while it was under construction. He always loved police work, always authority. These things fit this most unusual man like a glove. Maybe it is a good thing that there are not many Luther Herron's made. Too, it is good that we had a few and that Lancaster had the original. Again, history of Lancaster and Bastin Lumber Company could not be written without a detailed outline of this lawman's life. When Luther died he lived at 202 North Third Street in Danville. The cause of death was prostrate cancer.

The location in Harrodsburg of Luther's shoot out with Sam Black and Walter Stotts burned down in 1990. It was a livery stable in 1905 and was so well constructed; it lasted until 1990 when it burned. At that time it was a pool room and a lunch room. It was the same Rosser building. This building went all the way from Main Street to Greenville Street. The city has made a parking lot out of it now. It is strange to go down Main Street and come, all of a sudden, on this narrow parking lot that is most useful. It is easy to find.

Luther's theater still stands at Garrard Hardware in Lancaster. The Bastin Lumber Company and Lancaster Depot still stand even if they have changed in size and appearance. The rest of Lancaster is much the same except for the changing of the names of the particular businesses.

In adding up the score, I suppose that Luther could put at least eight notches on the wood portion of his pistol. There were three unidentified in Harrodsburg, then Walter Stotts, and Sam Black in the dual, Bill Jones, who had resisted arrest in Harrodsburg, and John and Albert Masters over an election. After this number went to seven, he moved to Lancaster where he only killed one, being Robert Strange. From 1905 until 1922 and only one killing it seemed like a new, more moderate Luther. As far as I know, Luther never had to kill again. For some reason, I think that Luther Herron was glad the killings were over.

Going back to square one, if policeman George Pollard had not been shot by William Hubble in 1906, Luther would not have been in demand by the Lancaster City Council. Officer Pollard was forty-three when this tragic event happened. He left a wife, Mattie, and six children. In only two more years Mrs. Pollard died leaving these children orphans. The Pollards are buried in the Lancaster Cemetery in Section two.

On October 12, 1937 Luther Herron left this life. He was sixty-eight years old and lived a full life. He traveled paths that few would dare to venture in. On his grave in the Harrodsburg Cemetery it states that he served in Company F of the 2ND Kentucky Infantry during the Spanish American War. His grave stone had the outline of a police badge. It is in Section K, Lot 9, and Grave 2 of this beautiful cemetery. His wife, Margaret Noel Herron, and five of his children are buried with him.

Luther Herron shooting Robert Strange

Last home of Luther Herron
3rd street in Danville

Luther Herron 1870-1937

Luther's grave stone in Harrodsburg, Kentucky

Chapter 4

James I. Hamilton

Our Best Customer Just Got Shot

My certainty about the facts in the Hamilton dual:

Absolute knowledge have I none,

But my wife's brother's son,

Heard a plumber on the street

say to a policeman on his beat,

that he had a letter just last week

a letter which he did not seek

From a Chinese merchant in Timbuktu,

who said that his brother in Cuba knew

Of an Indian chief in a Texas town,

who got the word from a circus clown,

That a man in the Klondike had it straight

from a man in a South American state,

That a wild man in Borneo

Was told by a man who ought to know

Of a well-known society rake,

Whose mother-in-law will undertake

To prove that her sister's niece

has stated plain in a printed piece

That she knows a Braves pitcher

Named Old Bob Buhl,

Who knew all about the Hamilton dual.

About 12 o'clock noon, on June 23, 1923, Clay Johnson came running into Bastin Lumber Company's office in Lancaster and yelled Jim Hamilton just got shot and killed.

Bob Goff and Hob Bastin had just bought this small retail lumber business from Hob's father, Alfred in 1921. In those days small lumber yards had to watch their account receivables with great care. There was no room for losing a large account. Jim Hamilton was not only their best customer, but he owed the two young partners a lot of money.

Jim owned more property than any three people in Garrard County. This meant that he needed a lot of lumber, tin, hardware, and paint to keep this property up. He was, in fact, a dream come true for any retail lumber yard. However, he only paid once a year and that was when he sold his tobacco. On June 23rd, it was a long time before a farmer would get cash for his crop. At the least five months.

At first the partners thought that this might be a prank or mistake. After thinking about it for a moment, it seemed possible since Jim was a bit high strung and he had some enemies. He had killed several people himself and was feared by more than a few people.

Clay had just come from the Public Square and by this time had caught his breath and revealed his source of information. Apparently Guy Davidson had heard it straight from Henry Burton, one of the only eye witnesses to the shooting. A tenant of Jim's, Clell Poynter, had shot him over an argument about the tobacco crop. The incident had taken place on the farm known as the Beazley Place located one mile north of town on the right. Other than that, Clay suggested that Hob and Bob call the sheriff, James Robinson and find out the details.

By this time the phone at the lumber yard started ringing off the hook with small bits of information about the killing. Some suggested that Clell Poynter had bushwhacked Jim. Some said that Jim was just shot in the arm and would live. Some said that it was a dual between two men who had called each other liars.

Thomas Chappell had called someone and stated the he saw a tall man going by his home on Lexington Street that was dripping blood from his shoulder. Could this have been Clell Poynter? Over an hour had passed since the killing and rumors were filling the air waves. Hob had tried in vain to phone the sheriff. Next, he tried his old friend, Police Chief Luther Heron. While Luther was now serving as Game Warden, he would know as much as anyone. Luther did not answer his phone.

The next effort to find out details on this mysterious killing proved to be more fruitful. Hob reached Jim's brother, Henry Clay Hamilton, a real estate broker, at his home. Henry told Hob that in fact Jim had been shot and was dead. Too, it was his tenant, Clell Poynter who did the shooting about an hour ago. While he could provide no more accurate information, Hob might try the court house. It had been rumored that Mr.

Poynter had given himself up to the sheriff and was either in the local jail or in the court house.

So it was with the gossip and personal information about this famous event that happened in Garrard County. Every person in Garrard County on that hot day in June 1923 could tell you exactly where they were on the day that Jim Hamilton got shot. Just like forty years later in Dallas, Texas when President John Kennedy was assassinated, people could tell you exactly what they were doing when they heard the news.

The killing made the Danville afternoon paper, even though it was inaccurate information. It stated that there were no witnesses and no one person knew what the killing was over. To the contrary, there was at least one witness and it became well known what the shooting was over.

Hob's next call was to the court house and information was available. It seemed that it could be stated as a fact that Dr. Bill Elliott had been called to rush out to the Beazley Place and attend to Mr. Hamilton. However, when the good doctor arrived, it was too late. Jim Hamilton had been shot through the heart and had been dead for at least twenty minutes. The undertaker, W. O. Rigney had already taken the body from the corner, Judge G. M. Treadway. The suspect,
Clell Poynter had been taken to jail and the main witness, Henry Burton, was in the court house under examination. Such was the situation on this unusually hot afternoon in Lancaster, Kentucky on June 23, 1923.

Around one thirty on this early summer afternoon a crowd began to congregate around the jail house on Stanford Street. Sheriff James Robinson and Judge G. M. Treadway watched as the crowd started shouting and cursing the man accused of killing Jim Hamilton. As more and more people gathered around the local jail the two lawmen decided to transfer Clell to the Lexington, Kentucky jail. It might be too dangerous to allow a posse to form and assist the local authorities. Remember this was 1923. At about two that afternoon it was arranged to drive Clell Poynter to the downtown Lexington jail for safety reasons.

Even though Clell had bested the older gentleman in a dual, he did not get off Scott free. Jim Hamilton had shot the younger man in the shoulder with the bullet coming out his side. While the bleeding had stopped the pain was growing stronger by the minute since the excitement had waned. Now an automobile ride to Lexington over a bumpy road with no pain killer or medical treatment of the injury, Clell would have to wait until a Lexington doctor would examine and treat his gun shot wound.

Jim Hamilton and His Background

On December 3, 1860 Jim Hamilton was the first child born to Henry Clay Hamilton and his wife, Mary Poor Hamilton. Over a period of eighteen years the Hamilton's would have four more children that would remain close over their lifetimes. Henry Clay Hamilton Jr. was born in 1874, Will Hamilton was born in 1876, Hallie Hamilton was born in 1877 and Atha Hamilton was born in 1879.

We know that Jim's parents were farmers and inherited the agrarian way of life naturally. While we do not know a lot about his early life, it is sure that he worked hard and had an excellent work ethic as a child. Too, he was a born Democrat and Southern sympathizer all of his life. He had no opinion of succession since he was born too late to have an opinion on that act.

Less than two months after the birth of Jim Hamilton, Jefferson Davis, Senator from Mississippi, rose up in the U. S. Senate and announced that all hope of keeping the Union together had been extinguished. In only four months after the birth of this popular Garrard County man the first shots were fired at Fort Sumpter, starting the American Civil War.

This cataclysmic event seemed to usher an omen on the future of Jim Hamilton. All of the traits of this terrible war in America seemed to bring out both good traits and bad ones in the character of this man. As we examine his life and death I think that the reader will understand what I mean.

He actually grew up during the time of Reconstruction. Since Kentucky remained in the Union, Jim did not have to undergo the adjustment of dealing with Yankee occupiers. Nonetheless, he would have to listen each day to complaints about the loss of slaves and ill treatment by the federal government. Still, Kentucky had it easy compared to the southern states.

Jim attended a type of elementary school and was proficient in reading, writing (excellent handwriting) and basic math. He would use these basic skills with great talent during the course of his life.

He got his first good job as a policeman on the Louisville and Nashville Railway. He was able to study at night and prepare for his law degree and exam. He did not have the money or financial aid to attend college and had to make the best of his time and means. The raw talent was there, and perhaps, it is a pity that he could not have afforded a formal education. Sometimes this moderates even the worst of men.

Jim was able to take this full time job, save some money, and take the BAR exam and pass it the first time. He depended on local lawyers to tutor him and used their advice to his advantage. It is a little more difficult to become a lawyer now.

His first duties were to make sure hoboes and bums and tramps did not take advantage of the railroad with free passes. This job gave him the authority that he craved. Along with practicing law, this job gave him his first real niche in life.

From about 1882, he would serve the first phase of his professional career as a railway detective, lawyer, local marshal, County Attorney, and policeman. Each of these positions would have the theme of authority written all through its content. Jim loved authority and loved to administer it.

In about 1887, Jim Hamilton went to the Buena Vista section of the county to look at farm land and visit cousins. There, he found a beautiful young lady who came from a nice family. This young lady turned his heart and he married Judith Hackley after a short courtship. The ceremony was performed by Rev. Benton Cook and attended by family on both sides. Judith had a sister, Clara, who remained very close, the rest of their lives. In fact, I obtained much of my information about this couple by reading their correspondence when the Hamilton's took annual trips to Mississippi and Louisiana. Clara has a daughter, Judith Shearer, who has been most helpful with information about this attractive couple.

Jim had no trouble in fulfilling the demands of his vocation. Early in his tenure of local marshal, he had to arrest a man who was armed and drunk at the old Mason Hotel. Joe Turner became Jim's victim by refusing arrest and actually attacking the young lawman.

At a young professional age, Jim took an interest in the local Democrat Party. His hard work made him a natural leader in politics. While Kentucky did not secede from the Union, it remained very similar to the old Confederate States of America in being heavily Democrat. While Jim did not try to force this on everybody, he expected every Democrat to stay in line on election day. There were allegations he used threats and force to keep the party on top. Since my forebears were Republican, we had little contact with Mr. Hamilton in this phase of his life.

In the early 1890's this maverick lawman killed his second victim at Crab Orchard Springs. It seemed that a man moved ahead of Jim's wife in a rough manner and refused to apologize. It has been told by several accounts that Jim beat him to death. I have no factual evidence of this, but tend to believe it because of my sources.

In 1895 Jim was joined by another gentleman who was as interested as he was for the Democrats to be successful. This man would be the antithesis of JIH. Where Jim liked it rough this man liked it smooth. Jim would not turn down a dare or fight. This new lawyer would find a way to circumvent both and still come out on top.

Joe Robinson had graduated from Transylvania College and obtained his law degree from Center in Danville. He started his own law practice in Lancaster and seemed, at first, to get along well with Jim.

Joe married Francis Collier in 1903 and settled down to work as a small town lawyer. He bought and became the editor of the local newspaper, The Central Record in 1910. This man was light years ahead of the town in civil rights for minorities as well as being a populist in political affiliation. While he was a Democrat with Jim, he interpreted that calling in a more liberal way. A conflict had been born. Due to the hard work of these two men, the local Democrat Party controlled the local politics until the Second World War.

Even so, Jim Hamilton was mentioned quite often during the tenures of Luther Landrum and Green Clay Walker as editors of the

Central Record. Jim made headlines even when he had a head cold. He had an appendectomy and the local paper covered it like a sporting event. However, when Joe Robinson took over the paper, Jim ceased to be covered except in the most important happenings. I feel that their problems started much earlier than most people thought.

In an interview with J. Wesley Lane (Mrs. Judith Shearear's father) Jim reportedly said that five men sat down with him when he went to bed at night. The five, being the people he killed up to the time. If this was true, he must have had a conscience that bothered him when these challenges came up. Ben Arnold was the man who revealed this source to me via an interview with Mr. Lane.

Lorainne Daniel, an ex-sheriff of Garrard County, also told Ben that Jim later killed at least six people in Bryantsville. This was called the Bryantsville Wars which were over politics and voting. While there is no actual proof of this, let it be made clear that everyone who knew this lawman-lawyer had a great deal of respect for him.

During the tenure as Jim was a postmaster, he added another notch to his famous pistol. On September 9, 1896, a Wednesday morning, rapid shots were heard coming from the Garrard County Court House. Investigation showed that Postmaster Jim Hamilton had killed Jim Knox, a shoe repair man. Too, he had wounded Judge R. A. Burnside in the fracas.

Knox was a shoemaker as well as a shoe repair man. He settled in

Lancaster in 1895 and bought out a stand where the old Mason Hotel (next to the alley on Stanford Street by the old Court House) stood. This property might be known as the Thompson-Morrow Hardware building.

It seemed that Mr. Knox borrowed some money from Jim Hamilton to buy tools and the machinery to repair shoes. While he gave a mortgage on the tools to Jim, the debt remained unpaid. Knox kept putting the matter off until Hamilton told him that today was not the first of April. In other words, he was not fooling about collecting the money. Knox was reportedly flippant in his remarks answering Jim. In fact, Knox said that he did not propose to be bulldozed by anyone about his finances. At this point in the argument, Hamilton turned and left Knox. This seemed unusual for Jim Hamilton.

About two hours later Knox showed up in Judge Burnside's office in the Court House and demanded that Hamilton be required to give him a peace bond. The Judge talked to Knox for some time after which Knox finally said he would drop the matter and fix up the mortgage. Judge Burnside then left Knox in his office and went after Hamilton, telling him what Knox had said. The two returned to Burnside's office and just as they entered the door Knox jumped out from behind the door with a pistol in his hand. At this point the judge found himself standing between Hamilton and Knox. Knox got the first shot off and it hit Hamilton in the chest. Jim would go another 9,777 days before three shots from the pistol of Clell Poynter would pierce his body and send him to the grave.

Jim Hamilton, as always, was quick to respond and drew his pistol and began firing. Knox had the judge trapped between the combatants in the middle of the scuffle. Knox used the judge as a shield and fired the second time at Hamilton, but missed. Hamilton then fired three accurate shots that hit Knox in the head and dropped him to the floor dead. During the brawl the judge got shot in the leg and in the arm. One of Hamilton's shots that hit Knox in the head was thought to have hit Burnside in the arm.

After all was said and done the judge had been shot in his right arm just below the elbow which cut an artery and nerve. The bullet went through his right thigh and into his left leg just above the knee.

The judge was taken into circuit clerk's office where Dr. Kinnard quickly went about dressing his wounds. The injuries in the leg were not as serious as the one in the arm. The judge seemed to be in great pain. After his injuries were managed, Dr. Kinnard attended to Jim Hamilton. Knox's pistol was so close to the judge's coat that the bullet set it on fire.

Dr. Kinnard thought that Hamilton's injuries were not serious, but that the judge would have to convalesce for a while. The judge would go on to live another twenty-one years in good health. The shooting of this esteemed jurist was purely accidental.

For Jim Hamilton, it was kill or be killed. Judge Richard Burnside stated that he would testify to acquit Hamilton, even though he was indicted by the grand jury. Jim Hamilton stated the he was glad to be charged by the grand jury since it would clear his name of any crime. Remember, Jim was not acting as a lawman, but was acting postmaster. A few weeks later, as expected, Jim was acquitted.

In Shakespeare's Merchant of Venice the money lender, Shylock agrees to loan a sum of money to Antonio. The deal is that if Antonio is unable to pay back the debt by the due date, Shylock would be able to get a pound of his flesh. Antonio agreed to these terms since he had a great deal of wealth coming in on several ships in the immediate future. The ships somehow failed to make it on time and Antonio had to give up a pound of his flesh. He was saved by a ruling that Shylock could have a pound of flesh, but not a drop of blood.

Jim Hamilton told Mr. Knox that it wasn't April the first. He wasn't fooling. There would be other people who would do business with this self-made man who would, like Jim Knox, regret the day they were called on to pay with a pound of flesh. However, to be fair, Haselden and Conn would start garages with loans from this multi-talented entrepreneur. He gave them their only chance. Many humble farmers throughout the county would accept loans from Mr. Hamilton and pay them back and prosper. He well could have been the most popular man in Garrard County by the year of 1900. A riddle wrapped up in a mystery in the midst of a maze. Perhaps he was like most of us in that there was a lot of good and bad.

While Jim Hamilton practiced law during most of his productive life, he had a switch in careers about the turn of the century. At this point in his life, he spent more time farming and in real estate. He was so successful in real estate that finally he devoted most all of his time to this pursuit. He served one term as County Attorney and then seemed to go into real estate full time. Still, we see times where he would defend a criminal that might be so bad that he could not get anyone else to represent him. This is the enigma that JIH presents.

So, as a rule, one might say that during the Nineteenth Century Jim Hamilton's main profession was in the legal field and police work. The Twentieth Century showed him more into farming, livestock and real estate trading.

In February of 1901 Jim and Mrs. Hamilton made their first trip south to sell mules and horses. Generally, they would go together on a train from Danville to Memphis. While he traded some in south Tennessee, he mainly crossed the state line and bargained with folks in the Delta area of Mississippi. They would take a steam boat from Memphis south to several towns close to Greenville, Mississippi to do most of their trading. These farmers used mules and horses until the late 1930's. Jim took advantage of this and became an excellent trader. The couple would stay generally a month in the south each trip.

In an article in the Central Record dated June 1912, Jim offered to trade some ewes (female sheep) for horses or mules. He then would plan his trip the next winter to Mississippi to trade the horses and mules.

Even though this area might be the richest farm land in the world, the folk there were not quite up with trader Jim Hamilton. He seemed to have a wealth of talent for any type of business deal. Greenville is in Bolivar County, named for the revolutionary leader of several South American countries.

The steamboat would take the Hamilton's right up to the local levee and pick them up a week or so later and take them back to Memphis or further down the river to points south. Even though the Kentucky market for this type of livestock was slow, it was always active in Mississippi. In 1901, he sold a railroad car of horses that would ship soon after the Hamilton's returned home to Lancaster.

On December 4, 1903 Jim went back into the jurisprudence field and defended a young man charged with rape. A mob had formed outside of the city jail and threatened to lynch him.

Just as the mob pounded on the front door of the jail, Hamilton came across the street from the court house and stopped them. Jim was acting as County Attorney at the time and later had to prosecute the man. He was always for law and order and protocol.

In 1905, Jim placed an ad in the Central Record that pointed out that the folks in Mississippi needed horses and mules in a bad way. Later, after his trip to that section, he boasted of his excellent sale for that year. By this time, the Delta farmers knew the Hamilton's well. His wife

Judith's support and presence had about as much importance in these outings as did Jim's trading ability. It helps any man to have the full support of a wife.

In 1905, Jim got a serious injury when he got his arm cut while herding cattle. He developed blood poisoning. At this time, he was still County Attorney and seemed to manage both jobs very well. In my interviews and reading of the Central Record I have not found any charges that he slacked on his public duty. He had no patience with someone who was lazy and would not work. A work week to Jim was six and a half days. Please remember that during this time he was very active in the local Democrat Party.

During this period, Will Hamilton, his younger brother was the Circuit Clerk in Garrard County. Will married Naomi Hamilton in Danville on June 21, 1905. They would be the parents of two sons who would be well known in Lancaster, but for different reasons. The older son was named for his Uncle Jim, receiving the name of James I. Hamilton and was born in 1911. Later we will write about his extending the grudge of his uncle's shooting. This would be thirteen years after Clell Poynter shot Jim Hamilton in the year of 1936. Will's other son was named Charles and became City Judge during the 1980's.

Jim's wife Judith made the headlines of the local paper by winning riding prizes at the Crab Orchard Fair. Too, she performed as well in the Brodhead Fair. These fairs were more important in that era than they might be today. They were the center of everyone's attention since they had no television and few automobiles. It was their only outlet to pleasure. Later in Mrs. Hamilton's will, November 1950, we see that she bequeathed some of the silver she won to favorite relatives. Jim did not seem to mind that she stole some of the limelight.

In 1906, Jim's new rival, Joe Robinson won the Democratic nomination and general election for County Attorney. He succeeded Jim. I can find no animosity over this succession. Joe stated early in his tenure in this office that Jim Hamilton had made a fearless servant of the people of Garrard County and an excellent prosecutor. Wile there was not trouble with this transfer of office; I have reason to believe that Joe Robinson feared Jim Hamilton and this emotion would grow as the years would fly by.

In February of 1905, Jim Hamilton announced that he would run for Congress in our Eighth District. The editor, Luther Landrum said that he would be worthy of this office since he came up from poverty as a self-made man. Jim lost the election and faced failure for the first time in his life. At this point in his life he has eighteen years left to live. Perhaps that could have been extended if he had won this election. Being in Washington might have moderated his views and placed him with people of his ability.

He seemed to adjust well by placing more time and effort on livestock trading and real estate ventures. Too, he was always on the leading edge of philanthropy. In the spring of 1905 an event happened in Lancaster covered in another chapter. It had to do with the shooting of police officer George Pollard by a bootlegger. The officer had a wife, who died two years later and five children. Jim headed up a benevolent group that liberally donated to this bereaved family. Joe Robinson and Alfred Bastin joined Jim in this charity.

In 1907 when the trial for this bootlegger came up it was difficult to find legal council to defend him. Since he had just made five children fatherless, no one wanted to show the least amount of sympathy. Jim teamed up with the revered Lewis Walker and ably defended this poor character and got him off with life. It is a miracle that this man wasn't lynched. Knowing Jim, it is surprising that he would take such a case. This just delineates the enigmas of this man of strange character.

In 1907, Jim took the defense of criminals a bit further. He made public his attempt to parole Henry Reddick from the state penitentiary. Henry had been sent there for some crime about seven years ago. In cases like these, Jim seemed to be a man of mercy.

In 1907 there was a new business going up on Creamery Street. (Now named Hamilton Avenue for Jim) Jim and my grandfather, Alfred bought shares in a new creamery that was being built on that street. It was located where the Antique Mall is located today. The refrigeration room is still there today.

From 1906 through 1910, the Hamilton's took trips south each year. They visited Memphis, Greenville, Mississippi and then on to New Orleans. One year they traveled to Florida. One small town in the Delta that they stopped at was Benoit, Mississippi with a population of six hundred. All were employed in the crop of cotton. Some of Judith's post cards back to her sister Clara Lane, who lived in Buena Vista, gave interesting details about their trips. Perhaps this stately couple made about eight or nine trips to the Magnolia State. I am confident that Jim made enough on these trips to pay their expenses and then some. The trips seemed to end in about 1912 and seemed to be his main source of pleasure in life.

In 1911, Jim sold a bowling alley that he owned on the north side of the square to W. T. West (1854-1927). Other than selling insurance on the Public Square he would spend most of his time in the buying and selling of farm lands. Too, much of his income would come from producing tobacco and hemp and raising livestock.

In February of 1911 Jim sold Henry Hutchins a farm on Broadus Branch Road of one hundred fifty acres at sixty-five dollars per acre. Land was just starting to go up in price as the county would soon be facing the First World War.

In 1912 Jim had one of the worst accidents of his life when a horse kicked him as he was getting off his buckboard. His leg was bleeding and needed attention. He was confined to his home for several weeks.

In 1913 Frank Conn went to the Citizens Bank and asked for a loan so he could open a garage to repair automobiles and carriages. Too, he might start selling a line of new cars. Mr. Conn was a natural mechanic and would seem to be an excellent candidate for a small business loan. For those of us who knew and remember Frank, only venerable impressions would come to mind. The bank would not issue this man a loan. As he left the bank dejected, Jim Hamilton spotted him sauntering down the street. After a brief conversation and inquiry, Jim told this twenty-six year old mechanic to take a piece of brown paper sack to the cashier of the Citizens Bank and get his loan. Frank did and got the needed money. Banks do not do business this way now, but this story really happened. No one would want to say anything bad about Jim Hamilton in Frank Conn's presence.

This proved to be one of the wisest acts that Jim ever performed. Frank made good on his debt and Jim Hamilton had made a friend for life. Frank worked out of the small garage on the corner of Danville and Paulding Streets and died in 1985 at the ripe old age of ninety-seven.

Many people remember this good man today.

From 1913 on, Jim would buy farms like a young boy would buy candy. The more land he bought, the higher in value it became. I will list some of the farms he purchased and their acreage and price per acre.

In 1914 he bought the Alexander Gibbs farm on Kirksville Pike of one hundred one acres at seventy-seven dollars per acre. He bought the

Bingham Conley farm on Sugar Creek of fifty-eight acres at twenty-four dollars per acre and the William Clark farm on Kempers Lane of three hundred fifty acres at eighty-five dollars per acre.

By 1916, Jim owned thousands of dollars worth of land in Garrard County as assessed by the PVA office. One would imagine that the real value of this land would be twice as high by this date. In any case he paid more PVA taxes than any landowner in the county. Remember, the graduated income tax had just been instated by the Democratic President Woodrow Wilson. These people did not have to pay income tax so it is no wonder that some of them could get very rich quickly.

In 1917, Jim bought two hundred fifty thousand dollars worth of farms, but sold many of them at a profit while not having to hold them very long. The prices ranged between one hundred fifty dollars and two hundred dollars per acre. This was the middle of the inflation in land prices. For that day, this is a high price. Too, keep in mind that a farmer could raise all of the hemp and tobacco that his land would produce.

In 1919, Jim bought H. Clay Sutton's farm of two hundred fifty acres for three hundred dollars per acre. This productive farm is on the corner of Lexington Pike and Sugar Creek. This gives the reader some idea of how land prices escalated during this World War I era. The American and European governments from 1914 on demanded much of the American farmer's produce. From 1912 through 1919 America was in a spiral of inflation of all commodities.

On March 12, 1916 a sad day dawned on the Hamilton family. His lifelong friend and brother, Will Hamilton, died after a short illness. Will was County Clerk and left two boys, ages seven and five, James I. Hamilton and Charles Hamilton and a capable wife, Naomi. I might interject at this point that Naomi took over the Hamilton's insurance business and inherited the insurance maps of the city for the years of 1915 and 1929. These cartoon drawings of the layout of Lancaster are invaluable to the historian. Jim and his wife Judith did an excellent job in filling in as surrogate parents for these boys.

On May 8, 1916 Jim Hamilton got involved in politics with an act that would cause a split in the Democratic Party at the local level. A meeting of the locals was called to order at the courthouse to elect delegates to the state convention. This would ultimately nominate Woodrow Wilson for his second term as President. Joe Robinson started the meeting of local Democrats off by giving a long, high winded speech about the virtues of Wilson and how he would keep us out of the Great War in Europe. Jim got tired of listening to the same propaganda over and over and told Joe Robinson to sit down and shut up. My source told me that Jim was quite expressive in telling Joe to cool it. This brought out the differences between the formally educated Robinson and self-made Hamilton. This did it. From that day on they never spoke, even though they lived across the street from each other.

While Joe Robinson paid lip service to Jim, he feared and loathed him. Everyone respected this fancy lawyer that spit out excellent editorials each week in his paper, but not Jim Hamilton. From this date on, if a clash seemed imminent, Joe just backed down. Still, it burned on his soul every time this real estate agent that had dominated everyone else called his bluff. Perhaps this could have been a factor in Hamilton's death seven years later.

Later in 1916, Jim again surprised the locals by defending a prominent farmer, Sweeny Morgan, (1849-1936) in a case where the latter had to kill his son-in-law. Jim and Lewis Walker successfully defended Mr. Morgan but against the prosecution of Joe Robinson. Most of the time the local lawyers and county attorney's argue with each other in court until they are blue in the face, then they go and have lunch with each other and socialize. Not in this case. The put down earlier in the year was permanent damage.

When people see the mausoleum of the Hamilton's in the Lancaster Cemetery, they always ask how many people Jim killed. Absolute knowledge have I none! However, in an interview with J. Wesley Lane (1883-1972), the father of Judith Shearer, Jim confessed that five men sat down with him when he went to bed each night. My source is Ben Arnold in his interview with Mr. Lane. Just who those five were might be difficult to name.

In 1919 several happenings took place that has some interest in this life of this unusual man. A new tobacco warehouse was being organized in Lancaster and Jim and his rival Joe Robinson both were subscribers. On April 10th of that year the last livery stable closed in town. The passing of the horse and buggy era had closed in this sleepy town.

Demand for homes and property in this first post war year was excellent. The Three S Lumber Company and Bastin Lumber competed for houses that were going up all over town. While Bastin Lumber played second fiddle to the older company, my grandfather did quite well. Jim Hamilton being a good customer helped a lot.

In September of 1919 Jim Hamilton lost two good barns due to fire. The cause was unknown. He only had four hundred dollars worth of insurance on each of them, but had twenty five hundred bales of hay stored in them. Jim lost a similar barn the previous year due to fire. Jim's woes were starting to happen.

In March of 1920 Jim sold the Charlie Deen farm near Camp Dick for four hundred dollars and acre to Robert Gulley. Jim took the Gulley farm on Buckeye Pike on the trade. He said that he planned to sell that farm soon. The Gulley's still own this beautiful farm at the intersection of Highway 34. Jim also bought the Rankin property of six hundred seventy-seven acres in lower Garrard County for three hundred fifty dollars an acre. This was the apex of property value for many years to come.

Jim refused to sell a farm on Kirksville for a bid of three hundred twenty-five dollars an acre near Kirksville in Madison County. The bid was made by Shelby Jett. While not knowing about the final outcome of this farm, I fill that Jim should have taken the offer. On July 3, 1920 Jim sold the Robert Gulley farm on Buckeye Pike. He was fortunate to move this land as the coming deflation would soon appear.

On September 8, 1921 the Central Record stated that lightening had struck another barn belonging to Mr. Hamilton. This makes four that he has lost in the last four years. Too, a lot of farm gear and equipment was stored in the barns and little was saved. The paper further stated that the causes were thought not to be lightening in every case.

THE GATHERING STORM

The total land assessment in Garrard County for 1920 was $116,382,201 then, for the first time ever, went down by four million dollars in 1921. This would be a pattern for the next several years. Remember, land was the source of the government's revenue until the graduated income tax came into play during the 1920's. Land prices would have to be soft indeed for the government to reduce them this easy. Still, I have record of Jim Hamilton protesting how high they were. He had the most land, so he had to pay the most taxes. This would soon change. In town, Frank Conn had just raised his gas prices to twenty-five cents per gallon. Unheard of!

Up until 1921 there were two or three crops that moved the economy of the south. Tobacco, cotton and hemp were among the basics. Jim had his finger in all three. While he raised two of them in

Garrard County, he sold livestock to the Delta farmers in Mississippi. Too, he speculated unsuccessfully in Mississippi property. You couldn't say that Jim wasn't game.

In Garrard County we find that the tenant and cropper became a large group of landless, who, in order to eat, must turn to laboring for their more fortunate neighbors on whatever terms the latter offered. Up to 1921 it was a quick way to get rich if you owned a lot of land. During the Recession of 1921, tobacco, the main crop of Garrard County, sold for the lowest price in history, but our farmers had to buy manufactured goods at high prices that were set in the industrial North.

The First World War brought an unusual amount of inflation to products grown in the United States. A farmer could get almost a dollar a pound for his tobacco and could raise all he could manage. Quantity control and surplus was not dealt with until the Roosevelt administration in 1934. With this kind of return on his crop he could buy more land and raise all of the tobacco he wanted. Everybody wanted to get in on the get rich farm trade while land was still for sale.

The 1920's were about to change this way of investing. The farmer was about to experience difficult and frustrating times. Most other segments of the population enjoyed prosperity, but agriculture suffered from high costs of operation and depleting prices. Jim Hamilton enjoyed good times with his farm holdings between 1900 and 1920. This has been labeled the "Golden Era of Agriculture". Demand by a growing urban population for farm products increased. This brought supply and demand to an excellent balance more than any time in his life. There were no large surpluses.

The welfare of farmers depended upon the relationship between the prices of their commodities and the prices of non-farm goods that they might purchase. During this twenty years farm prices rose faster than industrial prices. My dad, Hob Bastin, told me that he was glad that he bought the Bastin Lumber Company from his father in 1921, since it did well in the 1920's. Not farm produce!

Jim did well and benefited from rising land prices in the years prior to the 1920's. As I scanned the Central Record each year between 1900 and 1920 each issue would gasp at the good buys that Hamilton had negotiated. Land went from about twenty-five dollars an acre in 1900 to one hundred seventy-five an acre in 1920. In short, Jim made good money just by buying land and holding it. There was a tremendous demand for food, fiber and tobacco.

The price of cattle also was going higher. He was an excellent cattle man. On the day of the dual with Clell Poynter, he met early with his good friend, Bill Lawson, to look at his cattle. He was quite proud of the cattle he grazed on the Beazley Farm, since it was the best he had left after the recession hit.

In 1920 prices of farm commodities changed radically. Agriculture prices began to slip in the summer and by the end of the year farmers were in a post war depression. Hog and cattle prices did not drop until November and December of 1920. By June of the next year they were down by fifty percent. Jim Hamilton certainly did not anticipate anything as severe as this. By 1921 farmers net income was down by half. Land prices tumbled and Jim was, for the first time in his life, in big financial trouble. Jim had bought some stock steers in October of 1919 at what seemed like a good price. After pasturing them during the following summer he placed them in a feed lot in September of 1920. When he marketed them the following February he took a big loss. The cost on his farm operation had not gone down. Prices on equipment, machinery, lumber, interest, and transportation had actually gone up. When he shipped livestock to Mississippi railroad rates had gone up also. Since he had gone heavily into debt to buy more farm land rates had gone up to about ten percent. This depletes land prices. In all of America, farm prices fell first, fell the fastest and fell the farthest.

The Citizens Bank of Lancaster had to invite Mr. Hamilton to an unpleasant meeting. I would not envied F. W. Champ, the president of the Citizens Bank, when he was nominated to be the one to go to Mr. Hamilton and tell him notes were due. Sell some of your farms, said Mr. Champ.

At this point I will have to give Jim Hamilton an A plus in his dealings with the bank and people in general. He did the right and honorable thing in this situation. He managed to pay his debts while not collecting a large portion of the debt owed to him.

The Beazley Farm on the Lexington Pike was one of his best. Certainly he would not want to split up this productive, well located farm. However, Jim had to come up with twenty thousand dollars soon or face foreclosure. He owned about seven hundred acres that included this farm and small farms around it. One can still see the old stone gates of the Beazley Farm. Just beyond them you can see the spring made on concrete about forty yards from Highway 27. This is part of the Spurlin Funeral Home property now.

The story has been accurately told to me by Woodie Leavell, that a Laurel County man, Henry Smith, came along one day and asked how much Jim Hamilton would take for about one hundred acres of land at the location of the Beazley Farm. Two hundred dollars per acre was the amount agreed upon. This amount of land was measured out and Jim had twenty thousand dollars to give to his creditors. The Smiths liked the place because it had a nice home, which is still standing, located front and center. In fact Hamilton built the house with a package from Sears and Roebuck. He bought the balance from Bastin Lumber Company. This house will play a part in the dual that took place in 1923.

Henry Smith, his wife Barbara and son Willie went back to Laurel County and packed up their belongings and moved into their new home. The last of this nice family, Willie, died in 1985 at ninety-seven years of age. He was a good friend to Alvin Brickey.

In the 1920's three large tobacco companies bought nearly half of the tobacco sold in Kentucky. Three meat packers bought over thirty percent of the cattle and hogs marketed. Six farm machinery manufacturers produced most of the agricultural machinery that the farmers had to purchase. What the farmer bought and sold was determined by others. If the price of tobacco drops from one dollar a pound (which it did) to fifteen cents a pound, the consumer is not going to buy more that he needs because of low prices. The reduction of price will not sell tobacco like it would land. If land goes low speculators will find a level to enter the market. But not with tobacco, surplus was the problem. Farmers could not pass their fixed cost on.

The drastic fall in farm prices in 1920 brought frantic demands that the federal government needed to do something to help the farmer. There were proposals for the government to purchase the surplus farm products and sell them at reduced prices abroad. Dump the surplus in other countries. The Harding administration gave the farm problem more attention than any other issue, except, perhaps, the naval treaties with the maritime countries. Farmers got a lot of sympathy, but little help. None of the Harding brain trust got to the heart of the problem which was surplus. The administration asked for voluntary reduction of acreage in tobacco and cotton. This was a joke. Look at my chapter on Goff and Bastin 1921 to 1943. No one would abide by a limit unless it was enforced in steel.

The Harding administration thought about placing a tariff on foreign products so they could not compete. This still did not address the problem of surplus. This was not addressed until the Roosevelt administration did so in 1934.

Jim Hamilton possessed a quick and inquiring mind that cut through the facts of a problem. He had the ability to attack a problem with unrelenting force. Sometimes he did not use his mind as much as his temperament. He was not a scholar even though he read and studied all of the time. He was a self-made man.

If I have painted a picture of Jim Hamilton that seems void of emotion I must correct myself at this point. On May 18, 1899 Jim handed his lovely wife the following:

His love for her never be ended,

How sweet it is when with hers can be blended,

The God who made the beautiful snow

Gave me the one whom my happiness I owe.

How grateful I'll feel when life does decline

My love and hers shall be closely entwined,

Sweet is the thought that death can not sever;

In the memory of each we shall live forever.

The last sleeping mound by the one of us living

Shall daily be found?

She will remember me with a memory so kind,

Her peer on earth no human can find.

When I look at my past, in the vision I see

A maid who loved, I know, only me.

The beam of her eye, the nod of her head

Is as sweet and gentle as and angel's tread.

I worship at this shrine as oft as I can

And long to be a worthier man

I beg even God on bended knee

To give her ever only me.

How true this poem turned out to be. After his death in 1923, Judith faithfully went to the Lancaster Cemetery and sat by his mausoleum and mourned. "The last sleeping mound by the one of us living shall daily be found." How true it turned out to be.

Clell Poynter and His Background

If Jim Hamilton would be the protagonist in this chapter, Clell Poynter would be the main antagonist. There could be no more of an antithesis to Jim Hamilton than Clell Poynter. They were direct opposites. Where Jim Hamilton was a professional man that made it rich, Clell was a tenant farmer who was poor. Jim Hamilton had no children of his own, while Clell had four at the time of the dual. Jim Hamilton was in the autumn of his life at sixty-three while Clell was thirty-five and in the middle of his youth. Jim Hamilton owned many acres of land while Clell worked for landowners. We could go on and on with this picture of opposites, but I am sure that the reader could easily grasp the truth in the preceding contrasts.

Clell Poynter was born on August 2, 1887, in the Crab Orchard, Kentucky area. At this time, my grandfather ran a general store that should have been very close to the Poynter home. While I have no evidence, such as newspaper clippings, letters or testimony of our families knowing each other, it would be highly possible. There weren't that many places to shop in Crab Orchard.

His father, James W. Poynter had married Mary Romans in 1860 at the beginning of the Civil War. Perhaps it was this national conflict that sparked Clell and his older victim to shoot it out years later. Jim and Mary had at lest six sons which included Ivor, Tom, Walter, Ora, Mason, Madison and Clell. Three of them served in the U. S. Army in World War I and all received an honorable discharge. Clell was twenty-nine when America entered the war and would have been a little old to have to serve.

I know little about Clell in comparison with Jim Hamilton. He was not written up in the local paper and did not own as much land as Jim did. He never killed a man before the dual, and few people were afraid of him. He grew into a tall, lanky man and was a very hard worker. While no one would push him around, he had no record of trouble. On August 28, 1906 he married Lillie Marshbanks in Cartersville, Kentucky. They lived close by in Flat Woods where he was a tenant farmer.

It is ironic that J. W. 'Will' Hamilton was the County Clerk that witnessed this marriage. He was the brother of Jim Hamilton. Little did Will realize that in thirteen years this man would kill his older brother in a dual.

At some point in his life he was able to save enough money to buy a four acre small farm and home on what is now U S Highway 52 or the New Danville Pike. The house is still standing and a picture is included at the end of this chapter. The property is now owned by Gordon Bourne.

On examining deeds of this farm, I found that it was most interesting that Jim Hamilton owned an eighteen acre farm that enclosed the small four acre farm that Clell owned. Perhaps a dispute over land could have started the schism. In any case, it does show that the two men knew each other before the year of the dispute. Both parties were very inquisitive type individuals and there can be no doubt of this. Armed with this knowledge I feel that this was the original point of contact between the two characters in this chapter.

In the 1920 census he and Lilly were listed as having two daughters and two sons. They were Margaret, born 1912, Ruth, born 1915, James C., born 1916 and William, born 1913. He later would have a daughter who was named Dorothy. We contacted Dorothy who lives in Florida and she declined to talk about this history.

One of Clell's brothers, Ivor Poynter, married a lady by the name of Mary Wilson. Their daughter, Everee Poynter, married Henry Alexander

Brown. They are both buried in the Lexington Cemetery next to John Y. Brown Sr. This couple had a daughter, Joan Luxson born in 1936, who has been very instrumental in helping me with the history of Clell Poynter. Joan would be a grand niece to Clell. Too, much information I gleaned about Jim Hamilton I got from his wife's grand niece, Judith Sherear.

Henry Alexander Brown died in 1974. He had a brother named Bascom Brown (1886-1973), who married Judge Henry Clay Cox's sister, Myrtle (1887-1957). Judge Cox was a good friend of mine and we discussed politics, history, sports and most everything on many occasions. We discussed the Jim Hamilton case, but I remember little about this since I had no idea about writing about it. Ben Arnold, the son of Cecil Arnold interviewed many old Lancaster folk in the 1970's and favored me with the notes of these annotations. Therefore, I made up for some of what I lost by failing to catch these people when alive.

About the only trouble that Clell was in came from his brother, Tom. In 1921 Tom got very angry at Clell over a crop that they were raising together. Tom, in rage, shot at Clell a couple of times. Clell got a warrant for his arrest, but withdrew charges out of sympathy for his brother.

While very little can be found in the Central Record about Clell Poynter, I have found several important things about this person that will be of interest to the reader. His grand niece, Joan Luxson a resident of

Louisville, Kentucky often visits the Lancaster Cemetery. While Clell is not buried here, the family has other relatives that are. She was kind enough to allow me to interview her and from this I will express her sketch of her great uncle.

Since she was fourteen when Clell died, she was able to remember first hand many things about him. She often heard him say that he regretted shooting Mr. Hamilton. He stated many times that he had nightmares about the event. While he had an excuse of having to feed his family, he rightfully pointed out that he had been warned about dealing with Jim Hamilton. Too, he knew that Mr. Hamilton was in a hard place himself in having to pay off a lot of notes. He knew that Jim Hamilton was big hearted himself and had signed many notes for tenant farmers that now were worthless. In other words, Clell realized that Mr. Hamilton was under a lot of stress. I think that it takes a good man to confess these feelings and circumstances after he has done something he regrets.

Clell was a good family man who was loyal to his wife and family. I can see this trait in the members of his family that I have interviewed. I talked with his daughter, Dorothy who is close to ninety, but remembered the incident well. So well, that she refused to discuss it with me any further. She expressed fear of coming back to Lancaster because of this happening, eighty-three years before. Other members of the family have expressed the same fear.

Please remember that the sheriff and county judge took Clell from the local jail to the Lexington jail to avoid a lynching. Clell did not come back to Lancaster except in very rare circumstances.

Clell first decided to share crop with Jim Hamilton in February of 1923. Since government papers did not have to be signed, it was more or less a gentleman's agreement as to split the proceeds from the crop 50-50.

It turned out that Clell gave half of his portion to Henry Burton, a resident of Lancaster. In other words, Clell only had a quarter interests in the crop. Jim Hamilton did not like Clell doing this, but could do nothing about it since there was no formal agreement.

One of my sources told me that Jim Hamilton was greedy in that he would let the tenant plow the crop under a verbal contract. Then he would observe when he had the crop raised to a point that there was not much else to do but top it and then harvest. He would run the tenant off with an excuse of incompetence. If one looks at the coroners report they will find that Hamilton asks Clell if he thought I had pulled off a crooked deal. Clell replied, carefully, that he did not look at it that way, but he must have access to his crop.

The last thing that happened before the killing on June 23, 1923, was a dispute between Jim and Clell earlier in that month. The two were arguing on the second floor of the court house in Lancaster and Mr. Hamilton's face turned bright red. He told Clell to wait a few minutes and he would be right back. As soon as he left several men told Clell that anytime Jim acted like that he was going after his pistol. As Clell looked out the upstairs window he saw Jim taking short choppy steps back toward the court house. Just as Jim entered the front door, Clell made way for the back stairs that descended into the clerk's office. This was a wise move since Clell did not have a pistol on him at the time. Jim did.

June 23, 1923, the Day of the Shooting

As the sun came up on that fateful morning in June of 1923, a heat wave had hovered over Central Kentucky for over a week. The Lexington Herald stated that the stifling heat would remain for the future. It was the good old summertime. In the nation's capital President Warren G. Harding was planning a trip to Alaska. He would be the first President to visit that state. The Cincinnati Reds played the Pittsburg Pirates in Cincinnati that day. The Reds were in third place in an eight team National League in 1923.

Clell Poynter was more likely to go to a Reds game than Jim Hamilton. He could have caught a train in Lancaster at the depot that would have delivered him to Cincinnati in time for the afternoon game. Too bad he did not go on that fateful day.

Clell Poynter rose from his nights sleep at about six am on that hot morning, while Lillie fixed his breakfast. He had her prepare a lunch for him since they lived so far from his work on the Lexington Pike, a distance of about four miles. Lillie, as usual, placed the lunch in a dinner bucket and they were ready to go. Clell was planning to go to the Beazley Place on Lexington Pike and chop the corn crop, since he had farmed out his portion of the tobacco crop to his friend Henry Burton. He had not planned to work at all on this oppressive Saturday morning. The temperature was supposed to climb to the high nineties and the humidity made it seem like one hundred ten degrees. However, Old Man Jim had been gripping about him not working and always wanted his workers to be there and at least look like they were working six days a week. Clell didn't want anymore run-ins with the old man since he knew well his disposition. Too, Clell was anxious to see his brother, Tom, who also tended a crop on the Beazley Place.

At about 6:30 am the couple started toward Lancaster in their buckboard aiming to arrive on Creamery Street (Hamilton Avenue) where Henry Burton's wife would deliver them to the Beazley Place for the morning's work. Henry and Mrs. Burton were ready to go as soon as the Poynter's arrived. The two men were delivered to the Beazley Place's stone gates on the Lexington Pike (they are still standing) a little after 7 am. Henry went straight to the tobacco patch just behind the Beazley house to plow tobacco. The small plants were about eighteen inches high and had been set for about a month.

Clell found that the door to the gear room was locked. Why? He had been promised access to the gear for the mules so he could have the crop plowed. This was part of the deal he had made with Mr. Hamilton. This is the first time he had seen the place locked up. He needed his equipment to harness the two mules so Henry could plow the tobacco.

Clell immediately went to the old Arthur Beazley house where Simon 'Buck' White lived with his wife Maggie. Buck was sometimes called Jim's bouncer since he kept all of the other tenants in line. In fact some people were as afraid of Buck as they were of Jim.

A little after 7 am Clell knocked on the door and when Maggie White opened it he asked for the key to unlock the gear room so he could hitch up the mules to plow the crop. Maggie replied that Buck had the key and he was over on Kemper's Lane cutting wheat.

Clell then found an old monkey wrench in the yard and immediately pounded the lock, but could not open it. It only jammed. Then, he jimmied the staples with the wrench and the door flew open. There lay the gears on top of what was left of last year's corn crop. Clell was glad that Maggie White was watching since Old Man Jim had accused him of pilfering corn.

Clell and Henry hitched up the two mules and the latter took them straight to the tobacco patch and started plowing. About and hour later Clell went back to the White's residence and asked to borrow a hoe so he could weed the corn crop. In about and hour Clell returned with the hoe and Henry returned with the mules and all tools and animals were put up in their original places. As Clell parted ways with Henry and the mules he headed toward the corn crop and saw Jim Hamilton and Bill Lawson in a buckboard heading straight toward him!!!

Jim Hamilton rose about 5:30 am on that fateful morning and had his usual breakfast of eggs, sausage, biscuits and hot coffee. After hitching up his buckboard, he journeyed across Lexington Street and picked up Bill Lawson (1857-1929). The two friends had planned to go to the Beazley Place to look at some of Jim's cattle. They traveled out the Lexington Pike and turned right on Sugar Creek Pike to enter the farm in that direction, rather than approach it from the Lexington Pike. It would be easier to look at the cattle from this vantage point as well.

As soon as Hamilton and Lawson reached the apex of the pike top of the first hill on Sugar Creek, Bill Lawson jumped out of the buckboard and opened the gate. There was a dirt road that led over the main portion of the farm and Clell Poynter was standing in the middle of this road. This was the first of the two meetings of the day between the two characters in this historic story.

While ex-sheriff, Bill Lawson was a good friend of Jim's he gave us most of our information about this argument leading up to the killing later that morning. He testified that Poynter started the conversation by admitting that "I have done a bad thing." He confessed that he had broke the lock and cut the staples on the gear room in order to get the mules hitched up to plow tobacco. He told Jim that he could not do his portion of the crop with the gears locked up.

Hamilton then replied that he had locked them up on purpose

since someone had been stealing corn and tools. Jim then told Poynter not to ever do it again. Jim scolded the younger man for meddling with his tenants. He stated that Clell had caused some of his tenants to turn against the orders that they had been given. Jim dared Clell to ever do this again. Clell then countered that he had never meddled or interfered with the tenants.

At this point of the argument Jim called Clell a liar. The argument had heated up to where both men were yelling and Bill Lawson thought that trouble might happen there and then. Perhaps neither man had a pistol at this time and tempers seemed to cool down as fast as they heated up. Jim then said that Poynter should go on and tend his crop and the gears would not be locked up anymore. Hamilton promised to feed the mules and work things out. Then, just as the trouble simmered, Jim expressed his anger about Clell subletting out a portion of the tobacco crop to Henry Burton. He accused Clell of putting Burton ahead of him.

Other sources have told me that Hamilton threatened Clell at this point and dared him to stay on the farm until he brought his pistol back to kill him. I do not believe this since Hamilton had enough sense not to warn anyone to prepare for such an event. It was obvious that Clell Poynter was not a patsy and any person of common sense would have better sense than do this. However, some of my sources said that Hamilton would lose his temper as he got older and make such statements. In any case, he scared Clell Poynter so much that he headed for town as soon as this meeting ended. This must have been about 8:15am.

As soon as this encounter was over Jim Hamilton and Bill Lawson drove their buckboard back to town. When this occurred it was a past 8 a.m. I do not know if Jim had a pistol with him at this time or not. If he didn't he picked up one at home as soon as he arrived. This was the last he ever saw of Bill Lawson or for that matter, his wife or any of his friends. He had about two hours left to live on this earth.

Clell Poynter also made the trip into Lancaster shortly after Jim Hamilton and Bill Lawson left the Beazley Farm. While I am not sure the exact time he left, I have understood by relatives of his that he went straight to Lancaster, turned west on the town square and headed to a location just behind where Quick Stop is located today. This would be about a half mile west of the Public Square. Since Quick Stop was not built at that time he went to the house just behind that familiar location where his father, James Poynter lived. He knew exactly where his father had his .38 Smith & Wesson pistol stashed. Since he had been threatened by his Boss before, he wanted to be ready. I do not know if his father was in agreement with this strategy or not. However, I do know that he picked the gun and went straight to Ball's Corner on the Square. This is named for the grocery store owned by Mr. Ball and the present location of the Apparel Shop at 37 Public Square.

At 9:30 a.m. or thereabouts, Clell met Joe Robinson on this corner and was quoted in the Coroners inquest as to the differences between himself and Jim Hamilton. The conversation was credited to A. K. Walker and quoted Joe Robinson as warning Clell to do what Mr. Hamilton wanted or to leave the crop and avoid trouble with him. The final advice to Clell was"...it is easier to get into trouble than out." At this time Clell Poynter left Ball's corner and headed out toward the Beazley Farm. I would judge that he arrived on the farm at ten am.

At 10:15 am Clell joined Henry Burton who had finished plowing the tobacco crop. They put the gears back in the gear room and threw the broken lock by the door. They were ready to go home and take the afternoon off. Up to this point, there is general agreement as to what happened.

Jim Hamilton left his beautiful wife and home (currently the home of Mary Adrian Davis 214 Lexington Street) and headed straight to the site of the dual at the Beazley Farm. Jim usually picked up Earl Clark (1910-1988) who was thirteen years old at the time. Earl would open and shut gates for about a dime a day. Too, he was a good companion for Mr. Hamilton since he had no children of his own. The Hamilton's loved children and often gave to charities that benefited them. I have noted this in an earlier portion of this chapter. Earl had been a bad boy for some unknown reason and was grounded that Saturday. He stated that he almost went with Mr. Hamilton anyway, but at the last minute decided to mind his mother. Lancaster folk have often speculated on whether or not the shooting would have taken place if Earl had been present. We will never know.

Jim Hamilton was a character that was always planning ahead. He feared no man and this is something the strong must inventory each year as they age. You are not young and strong many years. They go by fast. The tough work should be left to youth.

Jim reveled in politics and could bluff and hoodwink people with the best of them. He could dodge, evade and connive when necessary. He seemed to have an unconscious assumption of superiority. His ambition was so dynamic that it had little rest in his sixty-three years. One might go back and say that his life would best be expressed in Civil War terms since that was the year he was born. In any case, he possessed a quick and inquiring mind that cut through the facts of a problem and seemed to attack it with an unrelenting force.

This time he was going up against a younger man who was afraid of him, prepared for him and one who would not back down from him. He was a man who could not just walk away from a crop to avoid trouble at any cost. A man who had to feed a large family that was depending on his labor. A man that did not think like Jim did. A man that was shot at before and was used to threats and pressure. Perhaps, he was the wrong man at the wrong time. It does not pay to have people to fear you.

Each man expected trouble and for that reason was armed with a pistol. Mr. Hamilton had killed before and Clell Poynter had been under fire. Perhaps they were even when it came to this aspect of the dual.

Since he was a friend of the Hamilton family, perhaps my father held to the common view that Clell Poynter ambushed Jim Hamilton... This is what he told me. Hob stated that Jim Hamilton came to the Beazley place on the morning of June 23, 1923 and saw this tenant standing at the gate. For some reason my dad never mentioned the name of the tenant. He just stated that Jim ordered the tenant to open the gate. Since there were cattle in the field the gate had to be closed. Clell Poynter dutifully and grudgingly, according to my dad, closed the gate. There was no argument or scolding in this version. Perhaps an hour passed and when Jim Hamilton returned to the gate he had to stop the buckboard and open the gate himself. At this time Clell Poynter bushwhacked him.

There were several other knowledgeable people who believed this version of the killing. One of the most important sources that adhered to this position is John White, the son of Maggie White. Maggie was one of the two witnesses that saw the murder take place. He recalls his mother and father, Simon 'Buck' White telling him the same thing my dad told me that it was an ambush, a sneak attack. I interviewed Lewis Layton in the summer of 2006 at his home on Perry Rogers Road with the same conclusion. Several other sources felt the same way when they taxed their memories.

I will have to again state that I do not have absolute

knowledge. However, as I put the facts together I do not accept this point of view. First, the Coroners report stated that Clell Poynter got shot in the arm with a flesh wound. His great niece, Joan Luxson confirmed this and added that this would not be attended to until he was lodged in the Lexington jail later in the afternoon. She said that it was a wonder that he did not die from loss of blood or infection. How could Jim Hamilton get a shot off and hit Clell if it was an ambush? While it would be possible, it is unlikely.

Second, and most important, if one reads the testimony of Maggie White, made on the Monday after the killing, one would see that she agreed with the fact that the two men faced each other before the killing. She testified for the prosecution and against Clell Poynter. While she was a relative of Clell's, she gave testimony, if believed, that might get him hung.

In particular, she stated that she witnessed the whole debacle from her home which was the old Beazley Farm. She had a clear view of the fiasco, but at a distance of three hundred yards. She stated that Mr. Hamilton was in his buckboard facing her home. The other witness, Henry Burton gave the same, exact testimony. No difference at this most important point. The only two places in the Coroners report that they disagreed was the placement of Henry Burton and who went for their gun first.

Please remember that she and her husband were also tenants of Jim

Hamilton. They loved him and got on well with his leadership. They were devastated that he was dead. They probably were concerned about their future and the future of the farm that they worked.

The version that I believe comes from the Coroners report taken Saturday afternoon, June 23rd and Monday morning, June 25th. This is the only reports that we have left. Ninety-nine percent of the court hearings and testimony have been lost or destroyed. Ben Arnold, several investigators that I have employed and others tell me that there remain no more records of this affair. None in Frankfort and none in Garrard County court house. Believe me, they have been searched for!

The main witness was Henry Burton, a resident of Lancaster that owned his own property on Hamilton Avenue. He actually had one forth interest in the crop making him partial to Clell Poynter. They traveled to the farm together that morning and approached Mrs. White about the key to the gear room where the harness to the mules was kept. While he was not privy to the first engagement of the two combatants, he was a close, eye witness to the second and most important meeting of the two men.

Henry was examined and cross examined. His whole testimony was recorded in the Central Record on the Thursday after the shooting. His testimony differed from Mrs. White's in only his position in regard to Mr. Hamilton at the time of the shooting and who went for their gun first.

He stated, under oath, that he and Clell were walking straight west toward Lexington

Pike while Mr. Hamilton was in his buckboard coming straight east toward the Beazley Farm where the White's lived. As Mr. Hamilton approached the two men, Clell was on Hamilton's left side while Henry was on the right side. Remember, Mrs. White had stated that both men were on the left side of Hamilton. This is not an important difference.

Burton stated that he said good morning, Mr. Hamilton and there was no reply. Jim Hamilton then asked Poynter if he had replaced the lock on the gear room as he had promised earlier in the day. Clell replied that he had. Jim Hamilton then said not to let anything like that happen again. I would take this to mean that things had been missing from the gear room like tools, corn and other possessions of Hamilton. Not only had Hamilton called Clell a liar, but had implied that he was a thief. In Garrard County, in 1923, these were serious charges.

Hamilton kept the argument hot by going over the same ground that the two discussed that morning. He brought up the fact that Clell could not get along with his other helpers and were turning them against him. He went on to say that if he could not get along with these tenants and workers that he would have to get off of his place and give up the mules and crops. At this point it looks like Hamilton owns the mules. Earlier, it seemed that Poynter owned the mules. This is not too important at this point.

Clell Poynter now argued back with Mr. Hamilton. No one ever did this. What few tried were already in the Promised Land. Clell expressed again that he could not afford to give up his interest in the crop and that he had not received the help that had been promised him when the original deal was made back in February. He, according to Burton's testimony, had been promised teams, tools and aid that never materialized. In other words, Hamilton had not done all that he had promised.

Hamilton then said you don't mean to say that I have pulled off a crooked deal, do you?

The last words that were said before the shooting began were Clell's, no; I don't look at it that way.

At this time the one credible witness, Henry Burton, was standing to the left facing Hamilton and Clell Poynter was standing to the right of Mr. Hamilton. Clell was slightly at an uphill vantage point. With this insult to his honesty, Jim Hamilton went for his pistol at his side. Burton testified that he did not know if it came from his pocket or his buggy seat. But out it came. At that precise time, Clell, with his lunch bucket in his left hand turned like he might want to run away. However, as quickly as he turned, he pivoted around facing Mr. Hamilton and rapidly fired off five bullets into Hamilton's chest. Jim had gotten off one shot that hit Clell in the left arm and had exited through his left side. Immediately the venerable Hamilton fell to the floor of the buckboard with his feet hanging outside and his back facing the dashboard.

At this point, Poynter said I have killed him. The conflict was over. The most important event in the history of Garrard County may have just taken place. Garrard's most popular citizen and largest landowner was shot by a tenant farmer. Could this be the end of the story? No! Many more webs will be created out of this fabric.

Most of my material has come from the testimony of Henry Burton, a man who had a family, owned his own home on Hamilton Avenue and felt the need to move from Lancaster after he performed his court duty. He stood only ten feet or so away from the tragedy. There were other witnesses.

The most important was Maggie White, wife of Simon 'Buck' White. Too, she was the mother of John White who has helped me in this writing. Mrs. White was standing on her front porch about three hundred yards away from the tragedy. She testified that both Henry Burton and Clell Poynter were standing on Mr. Hamilton's left side. She later made it clear that only Clell Poynter fired a pistol. Just after the shooting, Tom Poynter, Clell's brother, came from the tobacco barn. This was not unusual since he was raising a crop on halves at the Beazley Farm.

Mrs. White asked him if Mr. Hamilton had been shot and he replied that no one had been hurt but a few people were fighting by his buckboard. Later, it was established that Tom arrived at the killing site just after Clell and Henry Burton started off to town. It did not take long for a crowd of over one hundred to gather.

The last witness actually did not see the shooting first hand. In the Coroners report, Henry Burton said that he first told Myrtle Smith, the ones that came from Laurel County and bought the one hundred acres from Jim and then told Jake Dunn, a black man who worked for Mr. Hamilton. Jake said that with the evidence he had that it was a dual instead of a bushwhacking. My source here is Johnson Price.

The Steps of Clell Poynter for the Next Eight Hours

Saturday, June 23 was a long and tiring day for Clell. After the shooting, his day had just started. Remember, he had been shot and no one had attended to this wound. He never gave thought to run and hide. He immediately headed for town to give himself up to Sheriff James Robinson. His first stop was the Smith farmhouse and at that station he asked Barbara Smith (1860-1938) if she had a phone. She replied that she did not have one. At that time, her husband, Henry (1862-1957) asked what's happening.

Clell's next stop was the Sutton farm that lies in the corner of Sugar Creek Pike and the Lexington Pike. Mr. and Mrs. Bill Kirby tore this house down when they build a new home there in about 1977. Apparently, there was no phone there. All the time, Clell was carrying the pistol while blood was dripping down from his side. Clell and Henry Burton got a ride in a buckboard back to the site of the killing.

The next site that Clell stopped at was the Chappel home. This was owned by Thomas Chappel (1857-1933) and is located at 253 Lexington Street. Daniel Cain has a termite treatment business and is the present occupant of that property. Still, there was no luck with the phone. While the Chappel's had a phone, they could not ring up the sheriff. Frank Broadus finally heard the news and phoned it successfully to Sheriff Robinson.

By this time, Henry Burton had caught up with Clell and they were closed to the town square. They met Guy Davidson and several others who were most interested in finding out news of this happening. From that point on, it was a straight walk to the court house. Sheriff Robinson met Clell there and heard his story and immediately locked him up.

The time was about 12:45 pm. A crowd had gathered around the jail and the sheriff and judge decided to bus Poynter to Lexington for safe keeping, while a coroner's inquest would be held in the court house.

Still, Clell had received no medical attention. Blood was seeping out of his side wound onto the RIO bus that drove him to his next destination. Finally, at about 4 pm, he reached his cell in Lexington jail and a doctor was summoned. He was in great pain while he was treated for the wound. No pain medication was administered. When Clell finally went to sleep that evening, he had passed the longest day of his life.

Following the Body

Dr. Bill Elliott, a distant cousin of the Bastins, tried to resuscitate the dead body of Jim Hamilton. Not possible. At least four bullets had penetrated the chest and one glance told the fifty year old doctor that death had set in. He pronounced him dead as soon as he made a close examination. He found that there were at least one hundred fifty people that now had gathered around. Summoning some of the stoutest to place the body in the buckboard, he allowed W. O. Rigney to take the body for embalming and preparation for the wake and funeral.

After Mrs. Hamilton was told of the tragedy, the body was taken to Rigney's office over the National Bank on the Public Square. By Sunday at noon, it was ready to deliver to his home where it would be viewed by family and friends. The funeral was held at the holding vault on the grounds of the Lancaster Cemetery. It was the largest gathering of people ever seen on any similar occasion. The crowd was estimated by many at fifteen hundred. Many were from out of town. The floral offerings were very beautiful and many. Rev. E. B. Bourland conducted the services which included three songs and a prayer.

While the Hamilton's already had a plot of ground picked out at the cemetery, plans for a monument had not been thought out. Usually, they never are. Permanent arrangements had to be made by his wife Judith. She loved the venerable gentleman very much in spite of his character. They had lived together many years and gone through a lot. She was heart broken over the death of Jim and it would be difficult to make decisions.

It took Mrs. Hamilton sixty nine days to negotiate and sign a contract with the Peter & Burghard Stone Company out of Louisville, Kentucky for a mausoleum. I do not know if she had counter bids and offers from various companies. I doubt it since there would be few concerns in the state that would have the ability to build such an elegant monument.

Finally, on September 3, 1923 she signed a binding contract with the above named company to build the vault. The exterior footings would be six feet deep with best quality concrete. The slab under the vault itself would be two feet deep. The dimensions of the foundation would be nine by fourteen feet.

The floor would be made of one piece of granite nine by fourteen while the walls would be three pieces of granite twelve inches thick and six foot five inches high. The cap stone would be one piece eight foot eight inches wide and twelve inches thick and extend beyond the crypt at least four inches. The roof would consist of one stone fourteen feet long by nine feet wide and sixteen inches thick at the center and taper down to four inches at the eaves.

The columns would be one piece each that measure sixteen inches in diameter at the bottom with a slight taper and a square cap at the top. The doors would be made of United States Standard bronze and would be the type as shown in the catalogue of the Detroit Mausoleum Works. The doors will fill the space in the front end.

All of the granite work is to be constructed of the best quality of Woodbury Vermont granite. The name HAMILTON is to be cut in square raised letters on the front edge of the cap stone at least six inches high. The mausoleum would be ventilated by six ventilators and provide above ground burial.

The Louisville based company agreed to complete this edifice by the first day of December, 1923. They failed to meet that date but Mrs. Hamilton graciously allowed them to complete by late January, 1924. The cost was five thousand seven hundred dollars. At this time, one could build a nice home with that amount of money. Until that date, the body had to stay in the holding vault.

In early February of 1924 when the stones arrived by rail at the railroad spur of Bastin Lumber Company they were unloaded by making a sled of lumber and sliding them the several hundred yards to the site of the burial. Albert Dudderar (1902-1982) recalled buying lumber from Bastin and Goff and making the slides.

I have visited the mausoleums of many famous people of history. The most famous was that of Lenin in Moscow. He died in 1924 at his estate just outside of Moscow, just seven months after Jim was shot. My wife and I have visited the estate and his sarcophagus at Red Square. The Russians will not disclose the secret of the embalmers, but a book was written about it. I suggest that anyone interested in his subject read the book, Lenin's Embalmers by Ilya Zbarsky.

While in Peking we visited the mausoleum of Mao which contained the essence of the personality cult of the leader. We could walk around each body in about ninety seconds. In both cases, we had to remain quiet and move at a slow gait.

Both of these tombs were much more elaborate than Jim Hamilton's in that you could actually see the body. Jim Hamilton had no such embalming. Mr. Rigney was no match for Ilya Zbarsky or the Vietnamese that handled Mao. He didn't even try.

The closest monument to the Hamilton grave would be in the Novodevichiy Cemetery in Central Moscow. The famous Russian premier, Nikita Khruschev is buried here in a tombstone that consists of black and white marble. The white stands for the good he did by breaking the traditions of Stalin and black represents the evil he carried out in executing thousands during the purges.

The last monument that I will mention is the one of Karl Marx in Highgate Cemetery in London, England. It consists of a large bust of Marx and inscription Workers of the World, Unite. Too, this monument is about the size of Hamilton's.

Cartoon drawing of the
Hamilton-Poynter dual with
Henry Burton watching.

JIM HAMILTON

HENRY BURTON WAVING

CLELL POYNTER

Map of the Jim Hamilton 700 + acre
farm. June 23, 1923. on Highway US 27.

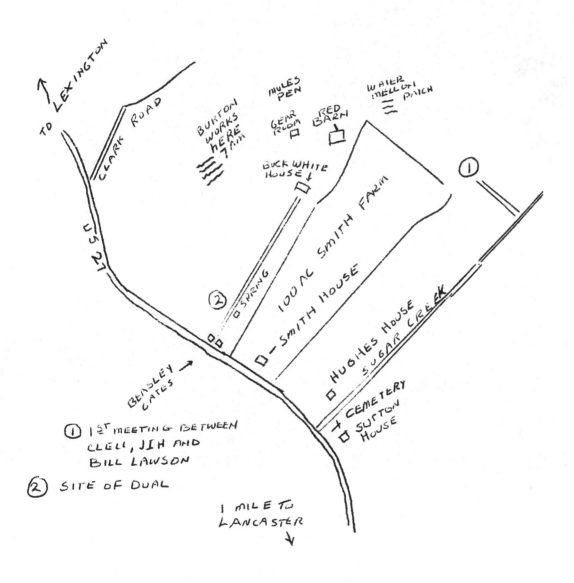

TO LEXINGTON

CLARK ROAD

US 27

BURTON WORKS HERE 7 AM

MULES PEN

GEAR ROOM

RED BARN

WATER MELLON PATCH

BUCK WHITE HOUSE

100 AC SMITH FARM

SMITH HOUSE

SPRING

①

②

BEASLEY GATES

HUGHES HOUSE

SUGAR CREEK

CEMETERY

SUTTON HOUSE

① 1ST MEETING BETWEEN CLELL, JIH AND BILL LAWSON

② SITE OF DUAL

1 MILE TO LANCASTER

John White and Hal Bastin 2007 in Bastin Lumber Co.
John is the son of Maggie White, the second witness in
the Hamilton dual.

Maggie White with grandchildren, a witness from the
distance in the Hamilton dual. John White Collection

The spring where Clell Poynter shot Jim Hamilton

Hamilton mausoleum, Lancaster Cemetery

L to R-Judith Hamilton, James I., Charles Hamilton, Jim Hamilton in around 1920
Judith Shearer collection

Judge G. M. Treadway. The judge who made the decision to save Clell Poynter from a lynch mob, and moved him to a Lexington jail

Clell Poynter's house on Danville Road 2006

Clell Poynter's grave stone in Lexington, KY

Judge Richard Burnside who got shot in the Knox-Hamilton dual

Jim Hamilton on left trading mules 1910
Judith Shearer Collection

Jim Hamilton 1893
Judith Shearer Collection

Jim Hamilton 1885
Judith Shearer Collection

Jim and bride Judith 1889
Judith Shearer Collection

Sequel to the Hamilton-Poynter Duel

James I. Hamilton who was shot and killed on June 23, 1923 had a brother, Will Hamilton, who was county clerk. He was very prominent in his right and the father of two boys, James I. (named after his uncle) and Charles. Will became ill in 1916 and died shortly after leaving a wife Naomi, and the boys.

This sequel centers on the elder boy whom we will refer to as James I., in the rest of this chapter. James I. was born on September 28, 1911, making him twelve years old at the time of the infamous duel. A twelve year old boy is very impressionable and adults should be careful what is said and how it is expressed around children of this age. Many of us learn prejudice and intolerance at this age and find it difficult to shake it off later in life.

There is no question that the death of his beloved uncle, coming six years after the death of his father, made a lasting impression on the young James I. The elaborate mausoleum that was described earlier in this chapter was bound to have a marked effect on his young mind.

One would think that he would hold a grudge against Clell Poynter and his family. Perhaps it was because the testimony against Henry Burton for freeing Clell Poynter. No, James I.'s hatred and malice went against the lawyer that defended Clell and the man who hated and feared Jim Hamilton.

Practically every person that I interviewed for this chapter told of stories about the hatred between Joe E. Robinson and James I. Hamilton. I feel that this ill will between the two men climaxed in 1916 during the selection of candidates to the Democratic convention of 1916. As mentioned before, Hamilton told Joe Robinson to sit down and shut up! From that point on, Joe Robinson was afraid of Hamilton. This is no disgrace in that most people would be in fear of this dominate man.

A number of people that I interviewed have expressed the opinion that Joe Robinson just might have put Clell Poynter up to doing a job he wanted done himself. Bill (Tobacco Bill) Johnson, my father Hob Bastin, Lewis Layton and others expressed the point of view that it was common belief that this description of the episode just might be true. No absolute knowledge. It was true that little James I. had heard this version of the killing many times.

It is also a fact that after Will Hamilton died in 1916, Jim Hamilton and his wife Judith took the two boys under their wings and spent a lot of quality time with them. When Jim got shot it was like losing a second father. One can imagine the impression that he had to deal with.

Over and over James I. would hear the blame placed on the editor of the Central Record. Time and time again the condolences expressed in the obituary were brought up as insincere. The family thought that Joe Robinson should have used someone else to write words of sympathy that he could not possibly feel. Too, blame was laid at the feet of Joe Robinson by some members of Jim's family. James I. absorbed all of this over a thirteen year period. Perhaps he had taken all he felt he could. Clell Poynter was out of town and no possible way to get at him. Joe Robinson lived just across the street from his Aunt Judith's home and it irked little James I. to see a new spring in his step as he walked to work each day.

Why did this man even defend Clell Poynter? Many people think he bailed Clell out. Two thousand five hundred dollars was a lot of money in 1923. Who put that much up for a tenant farmer? Where did this tenant farmer get the money to pay two of the best local lawyers and an expensive one from Harrodsburg? Many people have pointed to Joe Robinson. There is no proof of this, but rumors flourished.

Johnson Price told me that James I., who was now twenty-five never, missed a pep rally or ball game at Lancaster High School. He was interested in anything to do with Lancaster Green Devil sports. Lancaster High School played their first year of basketball in 1935 at Bastin Lumber Company. In 1935, there was no gymnasium at the school so they played in a warehouse that is on our property that stretched from Buford Street to the L & N Railroad tracks. At that time I think that Angle Sanders owned it. It burned in 1982 and Bastin Lumber Company bought it from the Taulbee estate.

My uncle, Ross Bastin, was mayor in 1935 when he was able to get a government grant of nineteen thousand dollars and back it up with a local bond issue of twenty-four thousand dollars to fund the first gymnasium for Lancaster High School. The gym would have a court layout of 44' x 76' and a 50'x95' floor. The WPA agreed to furnish the money only if the town would issue the bonds. The school had gone twenty-three years without a gym, so there were few opponents of such a deal. The Three S Lumber Company got the bid and had eight months to complete the job. They were successful. My uncle, Bob Goff bid on it, but was too high.

The gym was barely ready for the District tournament of 1936. Lancaster was eliminated early due to the newness of the team. Junction City and Danville made it to the final game that was held on March 6, 1937. Earlier during the school day James I slipped into the library and placed an Ivor Johnson pistol behind some books. He had read in the local paper that Joe Robinson would present the winning team with a trophy. James I watched the game until about three minutes to play, when he quietly slipped out of the stands and went into the library to fetch his weapon and seek revenge on what was done to his uncle thirteen years before.

When the clock was down to two minutes James re-entered the gym and approached Joe Robinson, who was sitting in the only row of seats under the visitors goal. Joe was seated with the trophy in his lap ready to hand over to the Danville team who had a comfortable lead with less than a minute to go. Superintendent C. H. Purdom was on one side of Joe Robinson while Walter Oakes and Chester Powell were on the other. Johnson Price had a vantage point, since he was sitting over the ticket booth and well able to watch the game and see what was about to happen to Joe Robinson.

James I. walked in front of this single row of spectators and approached Mr. Purdom by declaring that he should go outside and check on a suspicious character with a flashlight. After being rebuked, he persisted the second time by demanding Purdom do his duty. The educator told him that the janitor would handle the problem and to move. At that instant James I. pulled the pistol out from under a book that concealed it and pointed it at Joe Robinson. Joe saw what was coming and immediately reacted by throwing up his left hand. James I got one shot off that struck Joe in the left forearm just above the wrist, severing the artery and radius bone, tearing a gaping hole in his coat over his abdomen and finally, its force spent, the lead dropped into his pocket next to his heart.

The blood from the severed artery spurted for ten feet onto the playing floor of the gymnasium. Dr. Virgil Kinnard, who was in the audience, rushed to Robinson's side and applied a tourniquet made from a belt that was borrowed from one of the spectators. Joe was rushed to Dr. Kinnard's office where he treated the wound and then removed him to his home. The report said that he was in a great deal of pain and was very weak from the loss of blood, but would be expected to recover in due time if no complications developed. It did not help that Joe was a diabetic.

Immediately after the shooting, Hamilton was disarmed by Superintendent Purdom, Chester Powell, Walter Oaks, and a couple of the

Cormney boys. He was taken by the police to the home of his aunt, Judith Hamilton, across the street from the school building. He was placed under one thousand dollar bond by County Judge V. A. Lear.

According to spectators, no words were exchanged between Hamilton and Joe Robinson either before or after the shooting. No motive was advanced by the nephew. Mr. Robinson said that he did not know any reason why Hamilton should have shot him. I never had an argument with Hamilton, or even an unpleasant word.

After the shooting Hamilton was reported as being highly nervous and local physician Dr. B. Earl Caywood was called on to attend to him. One of the officers who took him to his aunt's home quoted him as saying that "I never could do anything right in my life, not even kill a man."

The grand jury met and indicted James I and set his trial for March 24. The date of his trial was set by Judge Alcorn with his lawyer, Pat Rankin of Stanford, looking on. He was released on three thousand dollar bond and placed under care of local doctors.

On March 25, the jury halted this ceremonial trial after thirty minutes and worked out a sentence, where he would be admitted to Central State Hospital for the insane. Both Dr. Virgil Kinnard and Dr. J.E. Edwards declared James I to be of an unsound mind. No doubt, Joe Robinson helped by showing mercy to this troubled young man. My understanding is that a deal was worked out that James I. would stay in the institution as long as Joe Robinson lived. Joe died January 7, 1942 and is the only man in the Lancaster Cemetery with two graves. One is a long slab that is not far away from where Jim Hamilton has his mausoleum. The other, is located eighty yards away from Mr. Hamilton and he is buried with his wife, Frances Collier Robinson who died in 1929.

Mrs. Robert Shearer, a niece of Judith Hamilton, told me that she visited James I at this institution and found that his care was found wanting. While not as bad as a prison, he was mishandled. While there, a Catholic priest befriended him and James I. converted to Catholicism.

In 1943, when James I returned to Lancaster he took up where he left off by attending school pep rallies, athletic events and hanging around the Walker Hotel. The local school children made fun of him, as always, but he seemed not to notice. In 1964, James I. passed away, which ended the grudge that took place in 1923.

cartoon drawing of
James I. Hamilton, nephew of Jim Hamilton,
shooting Joe Robinson in the Lancaster gym
in 1936. - HAL BASTIN COLLECTION

Chapter 5

The First Diversification: Henley and Ross

When Henley Bastin graduated from Purdue he mainly took technical subjects. I am sure of that this excellent university offered subjects on trends in economics and related subjects that might round out the young scholar. In any case, Henley was a thinking young man and could see that the phone company owned by an independent would not be a good, long term investment.

While still working as an engineer at the telephone company, he sought new ways to make a living. His first child, a daughter, was born in 1912. Then in the next several years, two sons, Charles and Henry V. were born. There would be no way to raise a growing family and educate them on the salary that he made at the Bastin Telephone Company.

In the early summer of 1912, Henley made a trip to Atlanta, Georgia to investigate a new product that was sweeping the nation. It was Coca-Cola. As I looked through the Record, I found the first Coca-Cola advertisement in 1922. Coke had advertised in big city papers long before this.

Henley was always an extravert. He was more interested in what went on around him than in his inner self. In no time, he talked to the lab of this new company and found that they would not share their secret formula with him. However, he was able to get some ideas on marketing soft drinks. This would be most important with whatever you might make and sell.

After experimenting with all kinds of fruit drinks and sodas, he came upon a concoction that he would call Mint-Cola. I have found the ingredients of this first mint cola that Henley blended as Lancaster's first soft drink. I can tell you who his business partner was in this venture. It was John S. Haselden. While John was much older than Henley, it was necessary to have a moneyed partner. As far as I know, this is the first business venture that the Bastin's made outside of the telephone business, but I am not sure how much success this venture produced. The Record stated that Coke had better watch out for this new, up and coming soft drink. I wish! After several years, the only reference that I could find in the Record was that they changed the site of production from the ice plant on Hamilton Avenue to a residence on Lexington Street.

I have seen a number of bottles of this unique product of Lancaster. They are dark brown and would measure about seven and one-half inches tall. The bottling company was called the Sanitary Bottling Company and the symbol H & B would be stamped on the bottom of the bottle. The first bottle that I owned was given to Henley's grandson, Charles Bastin, a resident of England. Charles visited me in Lancaster about three years ago and our family gave him the only bottle we had, since it was his grandfather who created it in the first place. I thought that I would find another by looking at local arts and crafts establishments or perhaps a local flea market, but no luck.

In September 2006, another cousin of mine, Jack Davenport, a lawyer from Chicago, paid our family a visit. He mentioned that he just about threw one away several years ago. "What?" I declared. "I will give you a hundred dollars for it." Jack then said that if he could find the bottle, he would give it to me.

On November 20, 2006, a UPS package came with this bottle in it. The only thing that I could send Jack was a picture of his grandfather, Ross Bastin's hardware store, which was located where the courthouse annex is located now. Jack's mother, Allene Davenport, had an antique shop in the front of my home on Campbell Street. This antique shop was located here for about five years until 1952.

If you have one of these original bottles, hold onto it. It will make a nice collectable. A July 1913 edition of the Record said that you should "Ask for Mint-Cola and other soft drinks bottled by Haseldon and Bastin."

While manufacturing this Mint-Cola, Henley thought that he might as well go into the ice business. At this time, few people had electricity, much less a refrigerator. I can remember when we had an ice box on our back porch in Cynthiana. I do not believe we had a refrigerator until just before World War II. While we were the last to get a modern appliance, the ice business was a big thing in Lancaster in 1915. Henley was on the cutting edge.

In 1913, July, Henley was called the Ice King. The ice plant was located on Hamilton Avenue where Cowden's factory was to be found. His brother, Ross, was in business with his older brother in this venture. The two young men stayed in this business for several years and at least made a good living. According to the Record, Ross attended seminars and learning conferences in Louisville that taught how to make a profit in the ice business.

As I read through the Record, I found that a Walker Coonhound was sold to a man in Texas for one hundred fifty dollars. Perhaps that was the business to get into. During this year, 1915, the first road signs appeared on the highways. Henley was interested in the new North-South highway being routed through Lancaster. It turned out to be called the Cincinnati-Chattanooga Airline Highway. Later, we know it as Highway 27. I have a feeling that my Uncle Henley got this highway routed through Lancaster rather than through Danville. He attended several meetings in Chattanooga lobbying for this very route. Henley was very civic minded and did this at his own expense. While others might have the same desire to show-case Lancaster, Henley had the education and aggressiveness to get the job done. People would listen to him.

While at Chattanooga, Henley tried to get the new Dixie Highway to route through town. Imagine how much early development we would have had if this had happened. It, instead, went through Louisville. By 1916, there were sixteen thousand auto license plates in Kentucky. The Hughes Brother Construction Company had been hired to lay crushed stone on the north-south road of Garrard County. This road would cost about one thousand dollars per mile. Progress was coming!

On August 15, 1915, the first Bastin Lumber Co. ad appeared in the Record. Alford Bastin had placed an advertisement in the paper promoting shingles. This was a small ad, but a start. At least two new businesses had already popped up from the sale of the phone company. More would follow.

Bastin Lumber Company had to compete with the Three S Lumber Company that was located just across Campbell Street. Actually, Earl French owns the property now on which this business was located. Examples of the type of house that the Three S Lumber Company built would be the three houses next to each other on Danville Street in Lancaster. They built 306, 304, and 302 about this time frame. Lonnie Napier and Robert Shearer live in these houses now. This competitive company built such good houses that they are still in style and fashionable.

In 1917, Henley Bastin and Ross Bastin made a major decision in purchasing the Electric Light franchise from the City of Lancaster. My two uncles promised good electric rates that would be twenty percent lower than any of the outlying towns. The Record said that the public would support the two brothers in this business venture.

We have already established that Henley was an accomplished electrical engineer. With his degree from Purdue, he could present an excellent resume, and his qualifications were excellent. While Ross did not have the technical training of his older brother, he had practical experience and was an excellent manager of manual labor. The boys signed a twenty year lease which would guarantee rates.

I do not understand why they did this. Alford had just dumped a business that would soon be killed by inflation. This inflation had become a reality in Mr. Cornn's phone business and was about to drive him out of business. They could see this right before their eyes. Wire had gone up, up, up. Why guarantee rates?

For the first few years, this new venture did all right. On January 2, 1918, they added a new water pump to the electric plant. This plant was located just across the street from the present location of my lumber yard on Campbell Street. It was just behind where John Mason had his cleaners. There was a pond in front of the electric plant. If you look at the block building of the cleaners you will see the block cracked on the South side of the building because of this pond.

On June 12, 1919, inflation had pushed this infant company to the brink of extinction. Now, the Bastin brothers had to ask the city for higher rates. While it is a private company, it can not just publish a rate that would show a profit to their company. Since the public depends on their product, they must get permission from the City Council. Too bad it doesn't run this way now. However, the government at another level does have to approve now.

Henley pointed out that they would be broke in a few months if the

Council did not allow them a higher rate. Henley prepared a statement that pointed out the rising price of coal, oil, packing supplies, and freight and hauling. He declared that he could no longer stay in business without an increase in rates.

Henley showed that his operating expenses were twenty-one thousand nine hundred twenty-seven dollars and ninety-five cents for the year of 1919. His revenues were sixteen thousand three hundred seventy-one dollars and thirty-six cents. The result would be a loss of five thousand five hundred fifty-six dollars and fifty-nine cents. No one could operate on these revenues. Unless the Council would grant the Bastin Brothers a higher rate, they would have to give up the franchise and take their equipment with them. I have the letter that they sent the Council. Henley had it notarized by Sue Shelby Mason. Henley told the Council that they should buy the franchise and run it and see for themselves the folly of a static rate.

On June 20, 1920 the Bastin Brothers tried to set aside their contract with the city. Either they got their rate increase or they would go home with their tools. Jim Hamilton, a friend of the family, did Henley a favor by bringing a suit against the brothers. This brought the problem to a head. Someone had to give.

The City Council actually asked these boys to refund all of the money that they charged to customers during the four or five years that they were in business. The brothers stated again that they could not go another twelve years without a rate increase. The city asked, "Why did you sign such a contract?" My Dad, Hob Bastin, replied that this was a good question. He told them that this was why Alford got out of the phone business and did not want anything to do with public utilities again.

By January 19, 1921, The Lancaster Light and Power Company had complete control of the electric utility. Henley has learned his lesson. This wizard of electronics now gets an excellent political appointment. He is offered and accepted the job of warden of the state penitentiary. Henley was in politics as a Teddy Roosevelt Republican as opposed to a William Howard Taft Republican. Roosevelt was much more of a progressive and a true liberal.

I am surprised how this talented uncle of mine could make such a switch in jobs; from objective in mechanical to subjective in administrative work. And with a great deal of success! I am quite proud of Henley since he would try many things and not give up until success came. Believe me, this was not easy street. Henley did not have it made as the Record stated a few years earlier. He did have an excellent paying, responsible job that was most difficult.

On March 10, 1921 Henley was named Superintendent of the State Reformatory. He resigned from the state Republican committee to take this job in order to be free from political influence.

In the October 20, 1921 issue of the Record, a liberal Presbyterian minister praises Henley for the humane manner he manages the prison. Dr. Steel, who examined the plant in Frankfort, did say that Henley had little to work with. The minister stated that Bastin needed more money and resources from the state to manage the inmates.

In 1924 I found the last mention of Henley in relation to this job in Frankfort. The Record stated that Henley was above politics and was doing a wonderful job. It was a difficult time to be the warden of a state penitentiary, since funds were scarce and resources limited. In any case this job was rooted in politics even though Henley did not play politics. He was fired from the job because of being on the wrong side in a political matter. His only comment was "Great! I will take my family on a Florida vacation."

In 1925, Henley packed up his three children and wife and drove to Ft. Lauderdale. I do not know much about the vacation, but remember my father saying that he bought up a small portion of what now is downtown Ft. Lauderdale. The trouble was that he was leveraged. He had too little down and too much borrowed. While this property was the only mortgage he had, as soon as the depression of 1929 came, he lost it all.

When Henley got back to Kentucky he had another job awaiting him. It was the job of Superintendent of Jefferson County Children's Home. The location was called Ormsby Village, which was near Lyndon, only a few miles from St. Matthews.

He was in-charge of three hundred eighty-one children in 1927 and the numbers grew until he retired in 1952. Basically, this was a reform school and difficult to manage. Perhaps it was more difficult than the state penitentiary. Too, this facility was probably the only integrated schools in the state at this time. Henley was light years ahead of his time. I remember him telling me that there was no such thing as bad boys and girls just misguided ones.

Since I attended Kentucky Military Institute in Lyndon, Kentucky, located just down the road from Ormsby Village, Henley would invite me over for lunch many times on Sunday. A large mansion and several servants went with the job. I was impressed.

The other member of the first Bastin Brothers was my uncle that I remember most, Ross Bastin. The Lancaster folks will remember him, since he was Mayor for fifteen years.

Ross ran the ice plant on Hamilton Avenue while working with the light plant. The Record tells that he went to seminars in Louisville and studied up on this crucial business for Lancaster, when the boys decided to get out of the light company because of low rates, Ross was interested in buying a hardware store.

The best store with the most inventories was the Haselden Hardware Store located on the square where the Courthouse Annex is now. Ross purchased it on November 15, 1923. Ross would be a natural in this business since he had the patience of Job, and knew the hardware business inside out.

I got to know this wonderful uncle of mine in 1965, when I came to take over the lumber yard. I was amazed at how much he knew about the small, mundane items of hardware. I would try to trick him by reading a current merchandising magazine and ask a difficult question. He always knew the answer.

I do not know much more about Ross in this venture. I do know that he, like Henley, was interested in politics and at one time was elected as a state senator. He was a Republican, but managed to put that aside when being Mayor or in business. I recall my father, Hob, telling me that Ross would help him work on the telephone lines as a boy. Hob said that Ross was the only brother that would actually go out and help him do the manual work. Since Ross' career at Bastin Lumber Company is covered in another chapter, I will move on to the next line of business which involved my Uncle Clinton.

Clinton would be the least known of the four Bastin brothers. He helped in the phone business and was in demand for a job in several local telephone exchanges. He took a job as head of the Houstonville exchange. He started his own clothing and dry good store on Campbell Street in November of 1923. He had a partner named Collier for several years before buying him out in about 1925.

In 1924, I came across an ad that Clinton had concerning Nunn Brush shoes. A good pair of high tops ran six dollars and fifty cents. This shoe today would be about ninety dollars. Apparently, Clinton handled brand name merchandise.

Clinton added costume jewelry and finally produce to his general store. He and Alford built the actual office that I enjoy now, but it originally was located just across the street from its present location. It was moved in 1946. My Uncle Clinton sold the business in 1927 and moved to Detroit where he met his wife, Adlaide. They had seven wonderful children who all turned out well. This family was raised in Decauter, Georgia. Other than visits, Clinton never returned to Lancaster.

The Bastin family in 1916
L to R-Henley, Clinton, Mayme, Hob, Ross

The Bastin family in 1936
L to R-Clinton, Ross, Allie, Henley, Mayme, Hob

Chapter 6

The Bastin Lumber Co. 1914-1921: The Alford Bastin Era

In 1912 Alford tried to sell the telephone company to anyone that might be interested. The trouble was that few had the money to buy a company that could not raise their rates unless the City Council would approve of the raise. If the council allowed it the people of Lancaster would protest. Alford knew this and so did everyone else.

J.R. Cornn, a gentleman from Tennessee was interested in buying the phone company. Alford immediately marshaled Hob and Ross to go out every road from Lancaster and repair the lines. They had about month to do this job which was necessary if the Bastin's wanted to sell the phone company. My Dad was about eighteen years old at the time and did not like to work as a lineman or at the switchboard. If this would help sell the company, fine.

Alford found out early that Mr. Cornn did not have any cash. He possessed a lot of rough lumber that he would trade for the telephone business. I am not sure how much lumber this proved to be, but my father had to unload it on Hamilton Avenue where Cowden's is now located. This was before any income tax, so there were no complications. Also, no tax benefits to either party.

Initially it would seem like a bad move for my grandfather to swap this income producing business that he knew like the back of his hand, for a bunch of framing lumber. When Alford realized that he saw a storm brewing between the council and who ever bought the phone company, it is easier to digest. In any case, Hob and Alford were in the lumber business and must learn it from the ground up.

I found out at an early age that my father owned two lumber yards and a portion of a third. Lumber business was all that I ever heard from morning to night, as I had to memorize my board footage tables from an early age. This was an immense help to me when I took over the Bastin Lumber Company in 1966.

The lumber that our family bargained for was rough lumber that one might build barns with today. While they soon added dressed lumber to their inventory, the rough lumber was the dominant product. At this time carpenters used it on houses as well as barns and bridges. While it was not as uniform and straight as dressed lumber, it was stronger and proved adequate, in house framing.

Alford was not actually green in his ability as a lumberman. He had operated a general store in Crab Orchard for eighteen years. In this store he sold many wood products that included railroad ties, lath for interior walls in home construction, and some framing lumber and so on.

As I searched for clues about this infant company in the Record, I found his first ad which featured rough lumber as well as dressed lumber. This was in 1915.

Alford broadened out by stocking shingles and all kinds of tin and several lines of hardware. Sherwin Williams Paints were looking for a distributor, so Alford picked them up. Now he needed a showroom to go with his merchandise.

In 1914, the year that the First World War started, he moved to our present location on Campbell Street. He used the first floor of my current home for a salesroom and the second floor as living quarters. This gave my grandfather about seventeen hundred square feet of floor space for merchandise paint, hardware, and related items, while an old barn was revamped to house the lumber.

In 1917, my father Hob was the only son to help with this lumber business. President Wilson had just done what he promised not to do. He declared war on the Axis countries. Hob knew that he would have to go into one of the branches of service. He chose the Navy since they seemed to need help in operating a telegraph. He had learned some of this in the telephone company business.

Hob Bastin enlisted in the Navy in 1917 and took his basic training at the Great Lakes Naval Base. While he was in basic training the Spanish Influenza hit the country. Dad told me that his roommate got sick one day, went to the infirmary the next, and died the next day. More soldiers died of this influenza than in the actual war. The Fields of Flanders would be safer than the congested training camp in Chicago.

Hob was able to pass all of his basic tests operating the telegraph and could decipher enough words in the time allotted to earn a trip to Harvard University in Cambridge. At this school, he had to get so many words per minute in order to stay in the program. If he failed, he would be sent to sea as a gunner's mate. No sooner than he finished the prescribed program, the war was over. Now, he was a twenty-four year old lad that would come back to Lancaster with a job at Bastin Lumber Company. My Aunt Mayme recalled that he was so proud to be dressed in his Navy whites and spats.

When Hob got back to Lancaster, he found that he had another clerk to help in this business. Bob Goff had married his only sister, Mayme, and because of her illness brought her back to Lancaster to live. In Lancaster they would have the assistance of the Bastin family to nurse Mayme back to health.

Bob Goff and my Dad became fast friends and worked well with Alford in this business. This arrangement would only last two years before youth clashed with age. The two young men had their own ideas on how to run a business and it differed with Alford. For one thing, Alford like to issue his friends credit until they sold their crop of tobacco. Bob and Hob did not like this idea. They weren't funded like Alford was and were not able to carry as much on the books. They liked to advertise much more than Alford. They would call in lumber and hardware salesmen and bargain where Alford liked the same old drummers that had been calling on him since his business commenced.

Finally, in 1921 Alford sold his interest in the lumber yard to the two partners. From now on it would be Bastin and Goff. The advertising became more prevalent in the Record and our company gave more competition to the Three S Lumber Company.

Alford was happy to be out of the lumber business and took on a new partner himself. He hired a cousin, Lenord Boone of Stanford. Their location was near the train depot and they would sell coal, grain, and feed and would buy farmers produce and poultry. Again, they had to compete against a Mrs. Witt who sold poultry on Campbell Street in a location very close to Bastin Lumber Inc current location.

I mentioned my grandfather in the first chapter of this book in regard to a strange happening. While he was in business at his general store in Crab Orchard in the 1890's something happened that seemed to worry my father a lot.

It started out when I was a child in Cynthiana and would ask my Dad why he did not have a gun in the house. Other children my age would point out the guns that their fathers had with pride. My father said that he had a bad temper and did not want a gun around the house in case he had trouble with someone. He further pointed out that if you killed someone, it would be with you the rest of your life. They would go to bed with you and so on.

I did not ask him any questions on this matter and, at that time, he did not elaborate. When I asked my Mother she said that his father, Alford, had probably killed a man in Crab Orchard many years ago. It was related to debt at his business, but she was not really sure. Too, she said not to mention it to my father since it was still very painful to him. Even though twenty years had passed, my father did not like to talk about it.

My Dad left Lancaster in 1924 and Alford committed suicide in 1925. Hob felt that it was because he had no one to talk with. When Hob was here in town, Alford could always come and pour out his soul to him. For some reason, Hob felt that he was the only one Alford could have this trust.

My first cousin, Willie Allene Davenport, was about nine years old at the time. She told me that she saw her grandfather go past the Garrard Bank with a rope in his hand only minutes before this tragedy happened. It took place in a structure close to where McDonald's is located now.

The Record account of this stated that he had no particular worries and few apparent problems. The family had a bad fire and many antiques were burned up, but he had adequate insurance. There was no apparent reason for the suicide at all.

During the 1980's this cousin of Alford's and mine, Lenord Boone, called on me at the lumber yard several times. I was so happy to make this man's acquaintance and fill in many gaps in my family's history. I was surprised to find out that he was in business with Alford and seemed to know Hob well also.

When I mentioned this possible reason for the suicide he

agreed. He said that while not having absolute knowledge he felt that he had killed someone in the distant past and it bothered him so much that he took this action. After putting the pieces together it seems to be the most reasonable answer.

Alford was a Christian man with high standards. Like my Uncle Ross Bastin, I have never heard any thing negative about him in the forty-one years I have lived in Lancaster. I hope that this is not true about him killing someone. It is possible that this worry influenced him to move from Crab Orchard in 1900.

Bastin Lumber Co. 1925

Chapter 7

The Bastin Lumber Co. 1931-1943: The Hob Bastin-Bob Goff Era

In 1921 Bob Goff and Hob Bastin polled their money and talents and bought the interest of Alford Bastin's Bastin Lumber Company. They had new ideas that their future advertisements in the Central Record would show. They wanted to sell dressed yellow pine lumber that came from the Deep South. The boards and dimensional lumber that they merchandised from Georgia and Alabama and Mississippi were out of long length pine and would allow them to sell lengths up to twenty-two feet and in some dimensions to twenty-four feet.

They met a new salesman by the name of Walter Freeman that worked for the Long Bell Lumber Company out of Quitman, Mississippi, that changed their way of doing business. Mr. Freeman worked as a young lad for this large company and in doing so, had a bad accident. While working in a saw mill he had his arm severed off by a saw. This put him in the office where he picked up many things that would have passed him by if he had stayed in the mill. He was enthusiastic and honest. The company liked these rare traits and promoted him to an outside salesman's job when he was older.

He traveled the state of Kentucky and met Bob Goff and Hob Bastin in about 1923, while traveling through Lancaster. Bastin and Goff bought what they could from Walter Freeman and would allow the relationship to go further over lunch. They talked about going in business together by buying lumber cheap in Tennessee and shipping it to Junction City, Kentucky to air dry. It would be too costly to buy a kiln to dry the lumber at this time.

They would use the Southern Railway to ship the lumber to Junction City and then after it dried for several months would ship it on another car via the Louisville and Nashville Railway to Louisville to sell.

Too, Mr. Freeman told of a lumber yard for sale in Cynthiana, Kentucky at a bargain price. A man by the name of George Hoskins wanted to sell in the worst way. He was losing money every year and wanted little for the inventory and buildings. It was located in a perfect location along a North-South Railway that connected Cincinnati with Atlanta, Georgia.

Hob made the seventy mile trip to Cynthiana to bargain with Mr. Hoskins in 1924. Sure enough, the price was right and everything was on go until the matter of money came up. Mr. Hoskins needed most of his money at closing. The two Lancaster partners could not swing the deal by themselves. Not to worry. Walter Freeman persuaded the Long Bell Lumber Company to loan the money at a favorable rate.

By mid 1924 the Harrison County Lumber Company was the property of Hob and Bob. Too, Mr. Freeman had two lumber yards to supply lumber to in this particular family.

While Hob liked to stay in Cynthiana and work his new business, Bob Goff liked to work at the yard the first half of the day and go out and buy property in the evening. The partners bought up at least six future Gulf Gasoline stations in Central Kentucky in the next few years.

In doing this, Gulf would rent the station from them for ten percent of the cost of the property. They would also have a codicil in the contract that gave Gulf the right to buy the property at ten times the original cost. Bob and Hob felt that this type of inflation would never happen so they agreed. In time, Gulf bought up all of the stations. A profit like this was really not so bad. I would take it every time.

In Lancaster, Bob Goff would try to get in on as much house building as possible. He would like to be a material man on new construction and new homes. Examples of this would include the Goff Apartment that burned in 2004 on the corner of Lexington Street and Maple Avenue, as well as Camp Dick Robinson School. While Goff did not get the contract on this school, he was the material man.

Hob, on the other hand, would try for farm business in Harrison, Fayette, and Bourbon counties. When my father arrived in Cynthiana there were two active house building yards in that city. Poindexter Lumber and Owsley Lumber were very aggressive and vowed to push him off of Oddville Avenue in quick time. My Dad had some fear that they just might be able to do that. He then went for the business that they ignored, the farm business. He would use his skills in barn repair and farm needs. Too, he would team up with roofers and offer specials on Johns-Manville shingles.

During this time that Bastin-Goff bought the livery stable that became the present City Hall. Clarance Wade used it as a garage to sell Oldsmobile's for about thirty years. The partners liked this kind of construction.

As I examine the Record during this time, the partners ran an advertising campaign that challenged the readers to build with the birds. Since birds would build a nest in the spring, Lancaster was challenged to do the same. Hob said that it would be in the interest of the whole community to build this spring. These houses needed to be well designed and attractive. Bastin Lumber Company could help you do both.

Now, in 1924 Bastin and Goff owned two lumber yards even though they had a large debt on them. They had to be careful who they credited and on what terms. While my grandfather owned the Lancaster lumber yard he was able to run credit on his best customers until they sold their tobacco crop. Hob and Bob did not have this much cash to manage this type of financing. They had to have their money at the end of each month.

While they inherited some excellent customers from Alford, they were in the process of weeding out the ones who wanted long term credit. Some of their best Garrard County customers fell in this category. Jim Hamilton, the man who owned the most land in the county, fell into this slot.

In Harrison County, Hob had one particular family, the Lebus, that owned many farms in Central Kentucky and would run up a bill to be paid once a year. He could not afford many customers, even though good, like this.

In 1932, Bob Goff and Hob made a trip to Casey County and bought a fifteen hundred acre farm for about four thousand two-hundred dollars. While this was an excellent buy even for those times, the reader must keep in mind that this was knob land with little bottom land to go with it. Any tobacco crop would have to be on a ridge and there were few of those to go with this property. Too, the government, the next year, gave tobacco allotments out by the acre. It was based not on how much land you owned, but on how much tobacco you had raised in the history of the farm.

In this case, little tobacco was raised on this rattle snake infested property. There was an excellent boundary of timber growing on the acreage that included all species of hardwood trees.
Very little coniferous trees were found on this location. This is where the immediate value of the property would be found.

Franklin Roosevelt had brought in the New Deal and with it many government programs. One of these was the tobacco program mentioned above. The Casey County farm that ran along Brush Creek was allotted one acre of tobacco! That's right! One measly acre! Or this is the way Bob Goff expressed it.

With all of this timber to harvest the partners got busy on setting up a saw mill run by steam. Soon, there was enough red oak to build a large barn that would have room for ten acres of tobacco. The first lumber cut on this farm would go into building this nice seven bent barn.

When the barn was finished Bob thought that it was far enough back in the bushes to raise an appropriate amount of tobacco. So, unbeknownst to Hob, Bob Goff had ten acres of tobacco set out. Bob felt that Roosevelt had it wrong. Anyone could see plainly that this boundary should have at least ten acres out of fairness.

In any case, no one would know about it in the hollows of Brush Creek. I personally can attest to the backwardness of this property. During the 1970's I would take my Honda 250, four cycle dirt bike and ride the gas line trails that circumvented the property. I saw at least ten rattle snakes during my travels over this property. Former County Judge Ray Wilson brought back at least three deer during the first deer season in Kentucky in about 1967. Believe me; it was out of the way. In the autumn of the year, it produced the most beautiful colors of yellow, red and orange assortment of leaves one could imagine.

However, you would be surprised how fast information flies when someone raises ten acres of tobacco, when only allotted one acre. The gossip spread to the court house in Liberty and Bob Goff was in big trouble.

The officials rightly caught this offense and the partners found themselves in court in Richmond, Kentucky. Why Richmond, I do not recall. My father explained to the judge that it was a mistake that would never happen again. For some reason, the judge let the lumber men off with a reprimand since the law had not been in effect but a short period of time.

Just as the judge pronounced leniency, Bob Goff called him a communist. It was not fair that a person could not do with his land what he wanted. Where was freedom? Hob immediately grabbed him and forced him out of the court house before the judge changed his mind. I think that this was the only problem that they ever had in their business dealings. Hob told his brother-in-law that they must obey the law, whatever it may be. Bob agreed to do this and they did well from then on.

The partners started to cut the timber on this large boundary and send it into Central Kentucky. While it was mainly used for barns and farm use, some house construction was utilized. They could get two by eights and two by tens up to twenty feet long. They could cut the four by fours for barn rails and eight by eights barn posts.

In 1936 a young man by the name of Tom Goeheagan came into Cynthiana from Oddville wanting a job. This tall, slim hardworking youngster would be able to do the work of three men according to my father. He would leave Cynthiana before daybreak in the summer and arrive along Brush Creek in northern Casey County before nine a.m. Workers at the saw mill would help him load his truck with about seven thousand board feet of hardwoods. This wood weighed about two and four tenths pounds to the board foot. While it was air dried, it still weighed more than dimensional house framing lumber today. Tom would be back in Cynthina just a little after noon and would eat while a crew in Cynthiana would unload his old Ford snub nose truck. My father had two of these that had gone around several times with the speedometer.

Tom would leave Cynthiana at one p.m. and arrive back in Casey County at three p.m. for another load. By six p.m. he was back again in Cynthiana with a load that he might unload by himself. This went on several summers so that the partners would make the best of a hardwood harvest on this valuable terrain.

In 1928, the two brother-in-laws got together with their salesman friend, Walter Freeman, and went shopping in Tennessee. They went on what is now US Highway 27 to timberland between Onita and Sunbright, Tennessee.

Walter Freeman would leave Louisville long before day break and meet Bob and Hob in Lancaster and drive to Sunbright. Their headquarters was a motel close by called the Glass House. I remember stopping and eating at this establishment on my trips to Atlanta in the early sixties.

They hired a man with a steam run saw mill to cut the hardwood boundaries that they had leased on land much like they had purchased in Casey County. In fact, they got the idea from the success that the Casey County property gave them. They wanted Mr. Freeman in on the deal since he could sell this lumber in Louisville.

While I do not recall the man's name they hired to cut and stack the lumber, I do know that he did an excellent, efficient job. He had ability in this line of work. As soon as enough lumber was air dried, perhaps in six months, he would ship it in a box car to Junction City, Kentucky via the Southern Railway. The three partners had leased land in Junction City to stack the lumber until it could be loaded on the Louisville & Nashville Railroad and sent to Louisville.

For two years the three partners made good money doing this kind of business. Mr. Freeman not only sold this lumber in Louisville but he was what is called a desk jobber. He was good at purchasing cars of western framing lumber as soon as they left Canada or the West Coast of the USA. He would buy them on the bumper, meaning that they would be loaded and on their way before he bought them. He might buy them while in transit say in Missouri. In another week they would be in Louisville and he would have them sold and routed to their buyer.

All good things come to an end. First, the gentleman in Tennessee started taking the cream of the crop for himself. He helped himself to the best twenty percent of the lumber in which he had no cost. He just took it. Bob Goff found out about it and informed his two partners. My Dad said that they met in Lancaster and traveled in Goff's, big, black Buick on to Sunbright to encounter this employee that had turned sour. Mr. Freeman just wanted to whip him while Bob Goff thought shooting would be more in line. My Dad advised caution. Too, Hob reasoned that while he was ripping them off, he still was making them good money. Stay with this man as long as he is making them money. Hob won out this time.

However, this did not last long. They had to go on another visit to Sunbright in about five months since their tallies of lumber began to dwindle. On the way, Hob found that his two partners were carrying pistols. Hob demanded that they stop before ever reaching the Tennessee line if they were going to threaten with this type of coercion. Hob reasoned that it is best not to use this type of persuasion unless you really mean to kill. Do not bluff with a pistol. The man they were dealing with was rough himself, and in that day and place, probably carried a gun himself. Too, they were dealing on his turf.

In any case, Goff and Freeman listened to the good council of my father. They immediately broke off business relations and ended their land lease. This was a good business while it lasted. Seldom will someone work for you, unsupervised, and be loyal in making you money. It just doesn't happen.

Goff and Bastin still had Walter Freeman buying and selling west coast and southern lumber by the car load. This was one honest man that Bob Goff and Hob Bastin could trust. Too, Mr. Freeman could trust the brothers-in-law.

Again, an economic downturn during the Depression stalled this jobber business. Remember, Walter Freeman did not have a warehouse to be burdened with. When the crisis came, he was able to liquidate the business quick.

My father would tell the story to a lawyer friend of mine here in Lancaster during the 1970's. John E. Smith of the firm Cox & Smith would go to lunch with my Dad and me quite often. Hob would tell John and me that we never had it tough economically. We never had to fight anything like the Depression of 1929 or even the recessions that followed.

He would say that Mr. Freeman was so smart that when the downturn came all he had to do was to close his office in Louisville. All he had was a telephone, a typewriter and a girl. I would interrupt my Dad and remark that I did not know that Mr. Freeman fooled around with girls. In turn, he would get mad, and state that was not what he meant by a girl. My father did not share the humor with John and me.

The sales of Bastin Lumber in Lancaster during this time might reach sixty to seventy thousand dollars a year. This was good for the 1930's. Finally, after the Second World War started, sales reached over eighty thousand. The partners were about to pay off the debt on their lumber businesses. My parents always saved as much as they possibly could in order to get ahead.

My Mother came from Bowling Green, Kentucky and graduated from what is now Western Kentucky University. Her father, Charles Drake, was elected to the County Judge's office in Warren County at least four or five times. She had been raised by parents that did not spend or waste anything.

Charlotte Drake arrived in Cynthiana, Kentucky in 1925 and resided at the Browning Boarding House on Pike Street. This was the same place my Dad stayed until they married and built a house. She taught school at Cynthiana High School from 1925 until the 1930's. When my parents dated it seemed that my Dad kept putting off marriage for as long as possible. Like most men.

My Mother had a sister that had a good job in the Coolidge Administration and would get Charlotte lucrative employment if she wanted it. Since Hob did not propose, she took the job, moved to Washington and started to work. This set a fire under my Dad's feet that few had ever seen before. He immediately called Washington long distance and lined things up for the next week. They were married in the Little Church Around the Corner. At that time it was a famous, small church in D.C.

They moved back to Mrs. Lizzie Browning's Boarding House in Cynthiana and went back to their original jobs. The school was happy to get her back as a teacher. She had not been gone long enough even for a replacement.

They were an excellent combination. She kept them in cash to live on by her school teaching job and he made the investments. I can remember him coming home one night when I was about seven and telling my Mother that they were out of debt! This was the first time that I had ever seen them cry. They cried just like babies. At first, I was afraid and did not realize that his was a goal that they had set years before. While they had a lot of debt, it was always manageable.

It depends on what kind of debt you have. If it is credit card debt then it is bad. Dangerous! They had no credit cards in those days, but still had installment buying. They did without. We were always the last in town to get any new appliances or TV's.

I learned a good lesson that night. I will never forget the quite emotion that they generated to me in that experience of debt liquidation. I vowed to try to pay all of my debts before I spent money for pleasure. I was told that a God in heaven helped them achieve this goal.

Not long after this, bad news came from Lancaster. Bob Goff had died of a sudden heart attack. We knew that he had angina, but were not ready for this happening. It was especially a shock to his wife, my Aunt Mayme. Mayme had depended on her husband for everything. In his way he was an excellent provider and protector.

It happened about three a.m. one Sunday morning, on December 19.1943. The obituary stated that he had a busy day at the office on Saturday. That Christmas was a very sad day for our family, especially his wife.

Even though this sorrow and grief, my Dad had to find a replacement to run this business in Lancaster. Cynthiana was too far away for him to commute. The roads were lousy at that time, as you can look at the tracks of Old US 27 when you leave Lancaster and go to Camp Nelson today. If you think that our 27 is bad now with all of the late afternoon traffic, look at what they had then.

This was right in the middle of the Second World War and my father was in charge of gas and tire rationing. He had to do this since he was too old for the war effort. He had just bought a piece of cleared property and built a Chevrolet Garage in the middle of town. I recall that the steel ceiling joist came from Birmingham, Alabama and were of poor quality. They were made of a low quality of steel since the best went for the war effort. The company that sold Hob these joist did not misrepresent the truth or anything like that. It was the only steel that he could get his hands on in 1943. The manufacturer told him that when a heavy snow was on the way put stud supports under each metal joist. When he did this, the stud was four inches off of the concrete floor. When a heavy, wet snow came the studs were so tight on the concrete that they could not be moved.

I remember people coming to the house begging for tires, gasoline and a Chevrolet car if possible. He would give none of the above unless they had the proper stamps. He would only give gas allotments to those who deserved them.

L to R-Bob Goff, James Neal, Hob Bastin. May 1921
This is now the living room at 201 S. Campbell St.

Hob Bastin and Raymond McNeese standing on the spot that Bob Goff parked his Buick in 1936 at the Cynthiana Lumberyard.

Bob Goff in 1937

DRY LUMBER WORKS BETTER

We buy only LUMBER which has been SEASONED---Then we stack this LUMBER in a dry shed, so whenever you are in need of

GOOD LUMBER

LET US HAVE THE OPPORTUNITY TO FIGURE YOUR BILLS

BASTIN LUMBER CO.

LANCASTER, KY.   PHONE 91   LANCASTER, KY.

WE HAVE WHITE OAK SAWED TOBACCO STICKS

WE HAVE WHITE OAK SAWED TOBACCO STICKS

WE HAVE WHITE OAK SAWED TOBACCO STICKS

1923 advertisement for Bastin Lumber Co.

Chapter 8

The Bob Goff Shooting

Bob Goff was born on Pearl Harbor Day, December 7, 1888. Only this was some fifty-three years before the Japanese bombed Pearl Harbor. Bob would live two years and two days after this infamous day. Being born to a pioneer family of cabinet makers from Dover Kentucky, he took an excellent job with Union Gas & Electric Company as a young man and would have had a promising future with that company if he had stayed with them.

Bob's tenure with the utility company lasted from 1912 to 1918, and then he felt the need to move to Lancaster, Kentucky to get help from his wife's family to nurse her to health again.

On January 20, 1914, Bob met my Aunt Mayme Bastin in Cincinnati, Ohio, while she was studying at the Cincinnati Conservatory of Art. Mayme was an accomplished painter spending many years at this hobby. I still have some of her paintings of flowers and rural scenery. Even though she was my aunt, I feel that she could have been an outstanding and famous painter if illness had not overtaken her.

Mayme dated Bob Goff and finally married him on January 27, 1916 back in Lancaster at the home of her father, Alford. As soon as the ceremonies were over they drove to Danville where they caught the train and took a short honeymoon trip. By February, they were back in Cincinnati with Mayme at art school and Bob with the Union Gas &

Electric Company.

Happiness and youth did not last long with this blissful couple. In late 1917, Mayme was stricken with a bad case of appendicitis at a point in history when this was a very serious illness. The German doctor that treated her allowed the bile to run throughout her system. From what I have been told by my family, this was an option that the medical profession had before 1920. I have been told several versions of what happened by different members of my family so it is hard to tell what is true or not.

In any case, I know that my aunt was a sick lady and the only recourse Bob Goff had was to bring her back to Lancaster to get aid from the Bastin family. I will have to give Bob credit for doing this when many would cut and run. I am told by reliable witnesses that he took excellent care of my aunt and to a point was and outstanding husband. Even though he was not interested in the church, he would accompany Mayme to the Lancaster Christian Church every Sunday. Again, many husbands would find this difficult to do. Too, he was kind to her in every way and attended to her needs when business problems might hinder in doing so.

In 1919, my father, Hob Bastin, came home from a stint in the Navy during World War I. He and Bob Goff quickly became fast friends. This was something unusual for my dad. It took a long time to get to really know him, especially in business as he did not trust many people. Many times he told me that Bob Goff was the only person he could trust in business.

In 1920, they worked for my grandfather, Alford Bastin as clerks. Both had the energy of youth and this did not last long. In 1921, they pooled what little money they had saved and bought out my grandfather's business, Bastin Lumber Co. Alford was happy to get out from under this lumber business since the competition was tough. The Three S Lumber Company got most of the houses in Lancaster at this time and Alford had lost interest in being a material man.

If you examine the local newspaper, The Central Record during this period, you see that as soon as Bastin & Goff took over the business the ads started to appear. Big ads! I do not really know how much competition we gave the Three S Lumber Company at this time, but I do know that the Three S Lumber Company did not place ads in the paper during this time. Too, I am sure that Hob and Bob Goff would have made money selling whatever, as they both were tight with money and could stretch a dime into a dollar even during a depression.

They would go out and buy small pieces of property and lease them to the Gulf Oil Company with an option to buy at ten times the original price. Not realizing inflation would catch them; all were sold in a matter of time. However, ten times the cost is not too bad. They bought one thousand five hundred acres in Casey County on Brush Creek in 1932 for only four thousand five hundred dollars. While it was all knob land with little tobacco base, it proved to be a smart buy.

I will cover some of the other stories about my Uncle Bob in a later chapter. I cannot recall too many things about him personally since I was about six years old when he died. I do remember him dressing well for family gatherings, but always seemed to have dirt under his fingernails. Perhaps a small child can only see up that far. Perhaps I just remember what my parents told me and mix that with things I remember. He drove a big, black Buick that was hot in the summer. I was placed in the front seat between my Dad and Uncle Bob. My brother rode in the back seat between Aunt Mayme and my mother. We went to Boone Tavern or Beaumont Inn in Harrodsburg most every month.

Bob Goff had big plans for the partnership with my Father. Some of this had to do with another businessman from Louisville that went well with those two. His name was Walter Freeman. Mr. Freeman had one of his arms cut off while working for the Long Bell Lumber Company in Mississippi. Hob told me that the company took him in the office and sort of gave him a promotion. Mr. Freeman took advantage of this and became one of their best salesmen.

He called on the Bastin Lumber Company in Lancaster and the Harrison Lumber Company in Cynthiana. Walter Freeman's business sense attracted Bob Goff and Hob. As mentioned in another chapter, they did well in a venture in Tennessee. Bob Goff was impressed with this one armed salesman and I think, tried to imitate some of his ways of doing business. In football, it would be called a hard nosed, smash mouth style play.

Perhaps if Bob Goff had lived past fifty-five, they might have leveraged more. He certainly did his portion of the work load in the partnership of Bastin and Goff. For this reason, when he passed away my father kept a normal work load. This was during the Second World War and Hob was in charge of gas rationing in Harrison County plus his obligation to both lumber yards.

Bob Goff did not like government control, especially the New Deal of Franklin Roosevelt. However, I should state again his determination to have every advantage when it comes to your property. Having a one thousand five hundred acre boundary of knob land with only one acre of tobacco allotment did not seem right. I feel that my Dad moderated Goff on government matters like this. He made him promise to always abide by the letter of the law. They had no more problems after this. Thank goodness the judge did not enforce the letter of the law on Mr. Goff.

Waddel Murphy would come to my lumber yard often and just talk football. He was an excellent football coach at Garrard County. He would have been recognized for his ability in this field if his health had not failed him. He coached in Cartersville, Georgia as well as Lancaster and knew football inside and out. For some reason, one of the times we talked, Bob Goff's name came into the conversation. Waddel said that he did not like Mr. Goff. As a child Waddel was playing in a barn located somewhere in the Cowden Court area. This whole area was owned by my grandfather,

Alford Bastin, and perhaps Goff was in charge of the farm and barn where Waddel was playing.

In clear terms, Mr. Goff told Waddel to get out and stay out. Little diplomacy was used in a situation where it might have been the best approach. A child will never forget mistreatment. This event would point out the gruffness in his personality. Either you liked Bob Goff or you were turned off by him.

Frances Spratt was a beautiful young lady that managed a beauty shop enterprise. Bob Goff did not turn her off. Many of the residents of Lancaster credit her with being one of the best in her business. Bob Goff rented the garage on Stanford Street to her husband, Bradley Spratt. Too, Bradley was a splendid mechanic with a lot of experience. My Dad mentioned that he was glad to have such a good tenant in the garage that would take care of the building plus pay his rent on time. This garage is where the City Hall of Lancaster is now located.

Bradley managed a garage in 1922 with a man named Ed Daughtery, who was considered an excellent mechanic himself. Considering that Bradley was only twenty-four years old when he started managing his own garage, one should be impressed. He was in on the ground floor with the automobile age. By 1923 he had bought out Ed, but kept him on the payroll as an employee. From what I have found out in the paper as well as testimony from my father, he was the leading mechanic in town.

By 1932, he was renting the garage that Bob Goff and Hob Bastin built on Stanford Street. In 1946, Clarence Wade would buy this garage from Hob Bastin and create one of the best businesses in Lancaster. Clarence made Oldsmobile the Garrard County automobile.

I have a picture of the town square and it is easy to see the sign of Spratt's Garage on this much used building. Bradley was able to get a jump start on the automobile business at a young age. Too, he worked for the Goodwin Brothers Motor Company in Lexington for a short while. He, like all of my family, was a member of the Lancaster Christian Church.

My Aunt Mayme Bastin, the semi-invalid wife of Bob Goff, did not like to leave the home except to go to church. Her recovery from appendicitis was going slowly and I am told that she looked and felt like a woman much older than her forty years. Bob Goff hired Mrs. Spratt to come to the residence to do his wife's hair. At this time, the Goff residence was on the second floor of my current home. The lumber business was on the first floor.

My understanding is that there were two initial connections between the two families. Renting the garage to Bradley and hiring Mrs. Spratt to do Mayme's hair. Soon, there would be a third.

I do not know the exact date when Bob started going with Mrs. Spratt. I am not sure that my father knew just when it started, but sure enough it did. I have been told that they parked at West Point at times. My nephew, Stewart Bastin, graduated from West Point in 1985, but this is a different West Point. Bob's West Point is located about a half a mile down highway 1295 as you go toward Richmond. There was a school located there and several of my best customers attended at that school in their elementary years. You would not think that something like this could go on in Lancaster without the husband finding out in a short period of time.

On or about November 19, 1937, Bradley found out about the affair and, according to my father, whipped his wife. The Central Record said that he threatened her. On the morning of November 19, 1937, Bradley expressed his feelings toward his wife in no uncertain terms, but enough to make her go to the sheriff, Tom Ballard, and serve a warrant for his arrest. As soon as Bradley had expressed himself to Mrs. Spratt by whatever means, he headed straight for Bastin Lumber Company with a thirty-two caliber pistol in his hand.

To understand the physical location of the events that were about to happen, one would have to realize how the lumber yard office was laid out in 1937. The brick building that is my home at 201 South Campbell Street came all the way out to the street. There was no front yard at that time; the front yard was created when my father remodeled the house in 1953. He actually chopped off about twelve feet of the old house to make a front yard for his sister, Mayme Goff. On November 19, 1937, though, the office extended all the way to the street.

At about eleven a.m. on that cool morning, Ross Bastin had gone to visit his sister about a family matter. He had just left the living quarters on the second floor of the house when he saw Bradley Spratt moving in short, choppy steps straight toward the office of Bastin Lumber Company. At this time, Ross had nothing to do with the lumber business. He did not get along well with Bob Goff and the feeling was mutual. While Ross, age fifty-two at this time, did not care much for his brother in law, he was about to save his life!

Bradley moved at a faster pace the closer he got to the lumber office. When he was about twenty yards away, it changed to a fast lope and finally almost a sprint. It seemed the closer he got to the business, the angrier he became. Unfortunately for Bob Goff, he met Bradley at the street entrance to the business not knowing what was to come. Bob did not think that his secret was out and perhaps Bradley needed information on the garage. Even though Bradley had taken a position with the Lancaster Motor Company and then resigned the Thursday night before the tragedy, he possibly could come to the lumber yard to talk business.

Bradley not only came to the lumber yard to talk business, but he came to the lumber yard meaning business! As soon as Goff appeared at the entrance of the office, Bradley took the pistol and began to fire. Click! The first shot misfired. Click! The second shot did as well. By this time, Uncle Bob realized that Bradley was not here for late morning tea. He turned, and like a soldier, went for the floor. Scrambling on all fours as fast as a forty-nine year old man could go. Bang! The third shot thundered towards Bob Goff and penetrated his left calf. Blood squirted all over the floor of the business. The fourth shot apparently missed. Bob Goff played dead instead of trying to get away. With two shots left in the cylinder of this pistol, this was a gamble at best. Bradley was mad and perhaps for good reason.

At this time, my uncle by blood, Ross Bastin, probably saved Bob Goff's life. He witnessed it all as he had just left the upstairs living quarters and was shocked by events as much as Bob Goff. Ross told me that he told Bradley that he had now killed Bob and would he please leave.

The front of the lumber yard was covered with blood and it is reasonable for anyone to believe a death had occurred. Later Bob Goff told my father that he felt dead since the pain was so tremendous in his leg. Too, he felt that Bradley might not be through with him yet.

For some unknown reason, Bradley felt his mission was accomplished. The feelings of hurt, anger, and remorse must have gone through his being. Perhaps, just perhaps, mercy might have had a small part to play in his decision to leave before he was one hundred percent sure that Bob Goff was dead. We will never know. But leave he did. I asked my Uncle Ross about this not long after I arrived in Lancaster in 1965. I asked if he was scared that Bradley might turn on him since he was a member of this family. Ross replied that it happened so quick that fear came later. He just wanted to get Bradley away from the lumberyard.

Bob Goff played dead until it was certain that Bradley was gone and would not return. He asked Ross if the coast was clear and when he found that it was he immediately put a tourniquet on the injured leg and stopped the bleeding. He had a presence of mind to calm his wife down by asking Ross to attend to her while he called number forty in Cynthiana.

In those days, it was no ten second phone call to get Cynthiana and his brother in law partner. After Central got Lexington and then Paris on the line, finally Cynthiana answered. Bob Goff was happy to hear Hob's voice on the phone. They had only few disagreements in their fifteen years in business, but never had they faced this. Bob had never discussed this affair with my Dad. I am sure he knew that Dad would not like it and would scold him for his folly. However, I feel that he had confidence that Hob would help him in any way necessary.

My Dad told me that when Bob Goff demanded for him to get a doctor to the Harrison County Lumber Company in Cynthiana he was shocked. Hob asked "what in the heck, did he want with a doctor in Cynthiana? Couldn't you get a doctor in Lancaster?" They had several good ones in Lancaster so why did he want this unusual request. For once in his life, Bob stood up to Hob and said "Just get one, I am dying." I will explain when I arrive; I will be there in about two hours. Just have a doctor there. I have been shot. Goodbye.

My father immediately called Dr. Brumback, our family doctor. With a two hour leeway it was no trouble to get this fine doctor to stop by his business and make his way the two blocks to the Harrison County Lumber Company on Oddville Avenue in Cynthiana.

Perhaps it was somewhat more difficult for Bob Goff to get into his big, black Buick and motor his way over narrow roads on Highway 27 to Lexington and then on to Paris and Cynthiana. Believe me, the roads were not much in those days. I know. I got car sick most every time I came to Lancaster.

You had to go through downtown Nicholasville, there was no by pass around Lexington, you had to go straight through Lexington traffic. Take Limestone Street and a left on Main then right on Broadway, which turned into Paris Pike. Go by Joyland Park and you would be in Paris around twenty-five minutes. Since it was his left leg that was wounded, it was sheer agony to put on the clutch each time the gear was changed. Can you imagine how many times you would change gears going the seventy miles to Cynthiana on the bad roads? By this time, blood was all over his floor board and his beautiful lather seats.

By one p.m., on Saturday afternoon Bob Goff passed by Stoll Field in Lexington. He was lucky that there was no game this week, UK was idle. That year, under C. A. Wynne, they had a typical UK year with a record of four wins and six loses. The week before, Boston College defeated them in Boston and in just a few days, Thanksgiving, Tennessee would defeat Kentucky 13-0. Bob had none of this trivia on his mind, he just wanted this act to go unnoticed and pass away. He would not press any charges against Bradley and hoped that his wife would not find out about what had happened.

At last he drove through the narrow streets of Paris and the final twelve miles to Cynthiana. The narrow road seemed to slim even more as he passed farm after farm when he entered Harrison County. Now was only six miles away from the jaws of death. The leg was starting to throb and jerk as it bled more and more. Would Hob have the doctor ready and willing at the Harrison Lumber yard? He had only told his brother in law to have a doctor ready within two hours. What if Hob could not find one? It was Friday afternoon after all. Both lumber yards stayed open until five p.m. on Friday and were quite busy on those days. What if Hob had customers and was busy? My Dad, years later, told me of the many things that plagued Bob Goff that day.

Hob had made adequate preparations for the arrival of this victim of folly. He had called Dr. Brumback, our family doctor, as soon as he knew Bob's life might be in danger. The good doctor was due to arrive before two p.m. and arrangements had been made to use a back room in the Cynthiana lumberyard where privacy could be guaranteed. The doctor would have something to relieve the pain and as well as to stop the infection. Sulfur drugs had come into use and Bob had confidence that if he could only make it the last few miles everything would be all right.

Back in Lancaster at this time, Bradley Spratt had arrived back to his home on Danville Street. His house was located on the south west corner of Danville and Paulding Street where Glenn May's Apartment is now located. Not knowing that his wife had procured a warrant for his arrest that morning, he dropped down in the first chair he came to so he could meditate on his drastic action. Bradley had never been in trouble with the law and was a first class citizen. He had always worked hard and always at church. The action was taken out of anger and righteous indignation. Still, Bob Goff had money and perhaps influence and his family might want retribution. He would not want to spend the rest of his life in jail. He was thirty-nine years old and had enjoyed freedom all of his life and now it seemed everything was ending.

At this time, Deputy Sheriff Tom Ballard arrived at the Spratt home and knocked at the front door. No one answered. He knew Bradley and realized that the charges were minor. In 1937 hitting or threatening your wife was not as serious as it might be today. Perhaps you would get a slap on the wrist and a small reprimand. Tom Ballard did not know anything about the attempted murder of Bob Goff, so there was no rush for the arrest.

Then Tom went to the kitchen and was admitted by Bradley. He told Bradley that he was under arrest and would have to go with him. At this time, according to Sheriff Ballard, the telephone rang. Spratt went into the next room to answer it and immediately a shot rang out.

When Sheriff Ballard went into the room Spratt was sprawled on the floor, dead, with the thirty-two caliber pistol still clutched in his hand. That shot could have been the shot that finished Bob Goff off if Ross Bastin had not intervened! The bullet entered the right side of his head and went all the way through, coming out on the left side. The Coroner, Sim H. Andersen, held an inquest Sunday morning and rendered a verdict that Spratt came to his death by a gun shot wound in the head, self-inflicted, with suicidal intent.

Bob Goff negotiated the last straight mile into Cynthiana and crossed one of the oldest covered bridges in Kentucky. Then down Main Street and after two turns he was on Oddville Avenue within sight of the Harrison County Lumber Company. With a left turn he drove to the side door where his brother in law was sitting with the doctor.

Blood was squirting on his car, on the weighing scales at the entrance to the office, and on Hob and Brum as they carried the patient to a back office for relief. Hob told me that it seemed forever before the doctor had retrieved the bullet from the calf of the victim's leg. Fortunately, the doctor had treated the wound before Goff had lost too much blood.

After a series of questions and few straight answers, the doctor left the two in laws to themselves. About this time, Ross called from Lancaster and told the two that Bradley Spratt had committed suicide. I do not know exactly the emotions of Bob Goff at this time. My Dad never went into this or if he did I do not recall what he said. I do remember Hob telling me that Bob's hair turned from black to silver in a few short weeks. With the coast clear, Bob Goff drove himself back home to Lancaster and joined his wife with a quiet night at home on a Friday night. He did not attend the funeral services of Mr. Spratt, which were held at his home on Danville Street. Nor did he walk back to the interment of his rival in the Lancaster Cemetery. By the way the crow flies; it would be a walk of two hundred and fifty yards. On this cold day in November of 1937, Bob Goff would have four thousand and twenty more days to think about what went on in the mind of Bradley Spratt on that fateful day of November 19, 1937.

When I think of this event in the life of Bastin Lumber Company and its place in the history of Lancaster, I wonder about the depths of forgiveness and the possibility that it might have saved the life of this troubled man. Now, in 2006, they lie only forty yards away from each other.

Only ten days after this shooting the partners, Bastin and Goff, made an important purchase of land just next to their existing property. They bought three small lots that measured 114' x 206'. This area was about a half acre and would become the main portion of the grounds that we have done business on for the last sixty years. In 1946, we had a major rebuilding program that will be better described in a later chapter.

Bob Goff getting shot

BEAUTY SHOPPE

Phone 170

Croquinole Permanents
$2.50 to $10.00

Spiral—$3.50 to $10.00

Combination Wave
$3.50 to $10.00

"Hair Cuts A Speciality"

Francis Spratt advertisement on a beauty shop December
23, 1937 in the Central Record

Bob Goff in 1924

Bob Goff and Mayme Bastin on their wedding day in
Lancaster, KY

Chapter 9

The Bastin Lumber Co. 1943-1965: The Ross Bastin Era

When Bob Goff died of a heart attach on December 19, 1943, the Second World War had been going on for two years. Millions of feet of lumber were used to crate overseas supplies and none of it came back. American industry had used more lumber each war year than had been produced. It was estimated that the countries needs in 1944 would outstrip production by three billion feet. Because of this, 'freeze orders' on lumber were unavoidable. In other words, building materials for house construction were tight.

Willie Hugh Sanders, the President of the National Bank for many years, told me that he built a house on Richmond Street during the war and wished that he had waited. He had to take second hand materials and had many material delays. While the Bastin Lumber Company of Lancaster and Harrison Lumber Company in Cynthiana had a lot of rough lumber harvested in Casey County, little of it could be sold to the public. Most had to go to the government.

When Ross Bastin got news that Bob Goff had passed away just before Christmas, he mourned his loss because his sister was devastated. He was the Mayor of Lancaster and had a nice farm on the Lexington Pike, which Holton Howard owns now. I think that there were about three hundred acres in the farm which lies good in the front, but somewhat rough in the back. Ross had been out of the hardware business for several years, but had good knowledge of both the lumber and hardware phases of the operation.

The Second War had entered the final phase of the conflict where it was only a matter of time before the Allies won. But what was the price we had to pay? How many dead Garrard County and Harrison County boys? My father had one man who worked for him that was in a German prison camp for almost two years. Too, he had a man that worked several years after he fought in the Pacific Theater of the war operating a fifty millimeter machine gun. He woke up nights reenacting scores of Japanese soldiers charging into his machine gun fire.

In 1944, Ross sold fifty-two thousand dollars worth of building materials at our lumber yard. This was good for war time and in Lancaster. During the last year of the war, he improved his sales up to eighty-six thousand. In 1946, the first non-war year he reached one hundred thirty-two thousand in sales. The distribution system had shifted from military to civilian markets. Housing went up for fifteen years after the depression and war ended. The biggest building boom in the nations history was about to take place. Nearly eight million servicemen returned home, ready to marry, further their education, and find good jobs. The GI Bill provided for a free college education and low cost financing for homes.

The demand for housing spawned the spreading subdivisions of new homes and brought prosperity and problems for lumber dealers. There was a big demand, but little supply. The Casey County boundary of timber had about played out. There was little left of this fifteen hundred acre hardwood forest.

Even though material shortages and rising costs plagued the industry in 1946, housing went over the one million mark for the first time. By the last half of 1947, the shortage of materials had dissipated.

Just after the war, it took six months to build the average house. By 1948, the time had gone down to four and a half months. Plaster was a portion of the house that took so long. It had to dry before you could put down your hardwood flooring. By 1950, drywall had taken the place of plaster and home construction quickened.

By 1948, housing prices had gone up eighty-eight percent over their cost in 1939. Food prices had gone up one hundred nine percent. Factory wages had gone up one hundred eleven percent and farm produce up one hundred ninety-one percent.

In 1947, the sales of Bastin Lumber went up to one hundred seventy-five thousand dollars, which would be about as high as my Uncle Ross could push them in his tenure. Too, a recession would hit the nation's building business by 1948. The next year would actually show some deflation.

I recall Ross telling me that many economists tried to scare him by predicting prefab-engineered housing as a wave of the near future. Either get on the band wagon or lose out. Dealers were urged to be prepared for this. Steel studs were promised for the near future. As far as I know, only one house in Garrard County was plagued with those before 1960. There is no substitute for framing lumber in house construction.

At this time, the area behind Cowden's started to develop. My grandfather had owned it, but sold it before home development came. A small four or five room house could be built in that subdivision for about four thousand eight hundred dollars in the early 1950's. By the late 1950's, the same house would cost eight thousand dollars.

In June of 1950 a war came again when North Korean troops invaded South Korea. The effect on the building trades was immediate. Now, non-lumber items such as asphalt roofing, cement, gypsum and nails were in short supply. Plumbing, heating, hardware items and wiring were difficult to obtain again.

However, the demand for housing was higher in 1952 than 1950. To counter this, the Truman administration placed a ban on houses having more that twenty-five hundred square feet of living area. Construction of schools, hospitals and roads were cut. Commercial construction took the worst dive.

Government restrictions were eased off in late 1952 and eliminated altogether in 1953. The Korean War ended in July of 1953. Since my brother, Bob Bastin was in Korea, we were happy that this had come to pass.

For some reason, 1953 was one of Ross Bastin's worst years. Most dealers improved after the conflict was over, but our Lancaster yard had a bad year. The year 1954 was even worse, but in 1955 Ross pulled his sales up to about one hundred twenty-two thousand dollars. One must remember that Ross was sixty-nine years old in 1953 and this was Lancaster. Lucian Colson was about forty years old and an excellent house builder. He owned Garrard Lumber Company and got most of the house building in Lancaster. Too, Feldman Lumber Company started in home building and was very competitive. There just weren't that many houses being built in Garrard County at this time.

Inflation was mild during the period between 1955 and 1965. It was about five percent a year during this period. Materials were changing; however, plaster was a thing of the past. Plastics were advancing into the markets. Drywall was now tapered to facilitate quick finish. Drywall mud that was pre-mixed was available. Windows were now pre-hung and arrived at the lumber yard ready to install.

My uncle got most of his mill work from Combs Company in Lexington. They were located on the site where the Lexington Herald is located on Midland Avenue. At this time, I was working in the lumber yard in Cynthiana and would drive up to Combs and pick up materials as early as 1955.

In 1955 it would be normal to use an inch and three quarter thick white pine door that would measure three foot by six foot eight inches, as a front door. It might not have glass in it. Ross would order the door from

223

Combs and have the brick molding and door jamb bought from another company. The hinges would come from Belknap Hardware out of Louisville. The carpenter would hang the door on the job site. This door only would cost about twenty-five dollars at the time.

By 1964, this practice would change. Combs Company would hang the door in Lexington with the instructions from Ross Bastin on whether to make it a left hand hung or right hand hung door. You might substitute a Douglas fir, Birch, or Lauan door, but the principal was the same. The evolution of the material business was ever changing.

Natural Gas and electricity were cheap in the 1950's and 1960's. Wood was poor material to make exterior doors out of since they expanded in the summer and contracted in the winter. The opposite would have worked out better. You need an exterior door to expand and fill all gaps to insulate in the cold months, but it was no big problem, since energy was cheap.

As energy went up drastically in the mid-nineteen seventies, a new door had to be marketed. The answer was a metal door. At first, they were difficult to obtain. I had to drive to Northern Kentucky and pick up a truck load about once a month. Finally, in about 1976, Combs Company carried them. They did not expand and contract like wood did and cost less.

During the 1940's and 1950's, Ross Bastin would furnish Douglas fir interior doors. Again, the carpenter would have to hang them on the job. During the 1950's Lauan doors entered the market. Soon Birch doors entered the market in Lancaster and were more popular with customers.

We entered the lumber business in 1912 when few products were pre-hung. Alford, my grandfather, would buy window jambs from one company, top and bottom sash from another and the metal sash liners and weights from a hardware company. He would have to put the window together at the lumber yard.

By the late 1950's this changed. Windows came pre-hung and a few years' later doors followed suit. While they manufactured plywood in the 1930's, it wasn't used in Lancaster in sheeting until the 1960's. Ross Bastin used one by eight number two yellow pine boards for sheeting. Lucian Colson, our rival from Garrard Lumber would use one by twelve Ponderosa pine boards in a sheeting grade. This was actually a number four grade. At that time, you could buy a box load of number four and pick the best eight percent out for finish grade lumber. After 1970, this was a dream of the past. If you bought number four, you got number four. Mr. Colson was a little quicker to use new materials than we were.

In Ross's tenure, from 1944 to 1966, he would use the one by eight board for roof and side sheeting. Other lumber yards would use the number four grade western pine which was as good, but not as strong. It just went on quicker and carpenters like the lighter western lumber.

Ross always got sand via a gondola railroad car. In fact, on my first day of employment in this business, March 1, 1965, we got a gondola car of sand in. Ross had hired three men to unload the car with shovels. They started at five p.m. when we closed and were finished at seven a.m. the next morning! I could not believe it. When Ross retired on December 31, 1965, Bastin Lumber Company never got a gondola car of sand in again. I could not find anyone to unload it for fifty dollars, much less the twenty dollars he had paid. Not twenty dollars each, but a grand total of twenty dollars. I got mine in via a tractor trailer truck that dumped the sand.

Ross was fortunate in that he had rail service during the entirety of his tenure. He did not use it as much as he should perhaps. Too, he did not buy in the quantity that we did years later.

Highways were improving during this time. The interstate highway system was started in about 1954 and would change long distance transportation. The improved highways would increase the range that customers would have to have materials delivered in quick fashion. Rail service would always be cheaper, but truck delivery could be much more convenient and on time. The L & N Railroad was installed in 1866 through Lancaster. Not long after this, one could take the train from Lancaster to almost anywhere.

Up to 1945, all of the Bastin's banking business was done at the Citizen's National Bank located on the North West portion of the Public Square. In 1952, this bank merged with the National Bank. During the Ross Bastin years, banking was easy and convenient. Ross and my father always could borrow as much as was needed at attractive rates. They did not have to borrow much since they always purchased between eighty thousand dollars to one hundred thirty-eight thousand dollars. Their accounts receivables did not vary much either. There was no need to borrow a lot of money.

In 1946, Ross blacktopped the whole lumber yard for nine hundred and fifty dollars. This is hard to believe. Too, he installed our own private spur to unload railroad cars at an expense of one thousand and two hundred dollars. This black top job was the very first job of Walden and Grubbs. In 1966, we got the same company to resurface the whole lumber yard at a cost of only one thousand five hundred seventy-eight dollars and sixteen cents. Not much inflation between 1946 and 1966.

In 1946, we moved our present office and showroom, which measured one hundred feet by thirty feet to its present location. Alford built this building in 1924 and was located where the parking lot for the CAP metal building is now. I sold this lot to CAP in 1986.

Tom Goeheagan built the two side sheds and cement house in 1946 to give us our present geographic set up. Tom could do the work of three men whether it was loading lumber or building.

House building in the nation continued their up and down movement, reaching a high in 1963 and a low in 1967. After 1961, there was no major recession until the 1970's. My uncle was aging and, according to him, was running out of steam. In 1960, he was seventy-five years old and his wonderful wife, Bessie Mae, was only one year behind him in age. The years of 1963, 1964, and 1965, his three closing years, gave sales over one hundred and ten thousand dollars each.

A small man by the name of James I. 'Buddy' Johnson came to work for Ross on February 2, 1948. This man, pound for pound, was about as good a worker as could be found. Buddy stayed on until 1967. Buddy could do it all. Ross learned to depend on this worker, especially during the last twelve years of his tenure. Lonard Murphy was hired January 27, 1951 and made an excellent employee for Ross. Lonard stayed until about 1967. Billy Coffey started on August 27, 1958 and stayed until 1966. These three workers were working at Bastin Lumber Company when I arrived on March 1, 1965.

Ross and Bessie May had one child, a daughter, who set up an antique shop and home decorating business from 1949 until 1952 in the first floor of my current home at 210 South Campbell Street. She featured Campbellsville Reproduction cherry furniture and assisted in advising on home decorating.

Bastin Lumber Company had moved the 30' x 70' store building from where the CAP parking lot is now to its present location on the East side of the street. Alford Bastin had built this store building in 1923 and used it with his son Clinton until he died in 1925. Clinton then used it as a general store until 1927, when he moved to Detroit. This building has been our sales room since 1946.

From 1944 until 1950, Tom Goeheagan and his family lived upstairs in my home and over Allene's shop. I do not remember a lot about the antique shop, but do remember my mother telling me that Allene was an authority on this type of furniture and decorating.

When the new highway came through Lancaster in 1952, an engineer by the name of Wendell Davenport met my cousin at Mom Blakeman's Restaurant on the square. They struck up a friendship and later married. They moved to Iowa then later to Illinois. Allene and Wendell have visited my family several times over the years. They both passed away during the year of 2005. They left behind three very successful children that live in the Chicago area. Sammy Davenport went into the insurance business, Jack Davenport, a lawyer, and Linda Davenport, a lawyer. Many older people in Lancaster remember Willie Allene. Jack Davenport was the cousin who sent me the Mint Cola bottle.

In early 1964, Ross' wife, Bessie Mae, became ill with cancer. Almost sixty years of marriage, and my father knew that it was only a matter of time before she would pass from this life. Hob knew that it would probably take the last bit of energy out of Ross's aging body.

On January 22, 1965 Bessie Mae Bastin died. My father was in Venice, Florida where he and my mother spent the winter every year. He asked me to pick up my brother, Bob, who also lived in Louisville and visit Ross to see if there was anything we could do. I can remember the sorrow that I felt for this man who had been married for so many years.

A year or so later, I asked my uncle how he felt without this wonderful woman being in the house and waiting at home when he arrived. Very stoically, he replied that this was a part of life and that he was prepared for it in some ways. However, he confessed that he was empty when he came home and she was not there. I wondered at that time how I would feel when that time came for me. Thoughts like this make your faith come alive.

I went back to work at the Kentucky Indiana Lumber Company in Louisville after the funeral. In only two months, my father called me again from Florida an asked me to thank Mr. Freeman for the temporary job in Louisville and move to Lancaster to help Ross finish out the year. I would take over the lumber yard at the start of 1966.

L to R-Bill Coffey, Kent Bastin, Buddy Johnson, Kevin Bastin, Hal Bastin
In March of 2006

L to R-Ross Bastin, Walter Bryant, Bill Coffey, Buddy Johnson, Lonard Murphy
In June 1, 1958

Chapter 10

Bastin Lumber Inc–1966 to Present: The Hal Bastin Era

On February 26, 1965, I woke up in Louisville with my few possessions packed and ready to move to Lancaster. The only problem was that the roads were closed because of six inches of snow. I had to wait until Monday, March 1, 1965 to make the two hour trip.

I moved in with my uncle at his residence on Hill Court. He had someone come to prepare lunch for us, the food was excellent. Later, I had to get supper on my own. I did not help much that year since Ross had his way of doing things and I did not want to get in the way. I did survey the way he did business and with whom. I found that he had no contractors that bought from him. He stocked only yellow pine framing lumber that was produced in the south. The contractors liked west coast lumber.

Ross continued the year with an average amount of sales. He showed a small profit in his last year of business as well as most every year he ran the business for my father. I hoped I could get along with my Dad as well as he did.

The main thing that I did in 1965 was to survey the Casey County property that I have mentioned before. The land came in three tracts that did not connect with each other. They mainly took up the knobs and ridges, but had few acres in bottom land. Out of the fifteen hundred acres, perhaps only one hundred acres were flat. It took about two and a half months to do this in a boundary that was full of rattle snakes and land poachers.

Jim Ramsey, the local funeral director, graciously flew me over the property just before I started to survey. I could see my property line was violated by people cutting my second growth of timber. This made it easier to get a court order for them to stop. My father had owned this property for thirty-five years and had not even set foot on it for sixteen years. This invites people to steal your timber and whatever else you might have. The only other thing we had on the property was a large seven bent barn.

We were fortunate to have at least three gas lines that ran from Louisiana to the east coast across this property. We took in more each time one of them crossed than the property cost us. This was one good deal that my father made.

After we eliminated the poachers, I sold what walnut logs we had to a buyer from Casey County. Three or four times a year I would take friends to this property and ride a dirt bike over much of it. Since it was void of any standing timber, there was not much use for it. I first had it for sale at sixty thousand dollars. As time went on, I kept raising the price until it was priced at one hundred thousand dollars by 1975.

I took my friend, Isadore Feldman to the property to see how much timber I had and what it might be worth. He confirmed what I knew, in that the timber was worth very little. While Mr. Feldman ran a lumber yard in Lancaster starting in 1937, he competed very little with our lumber yard. We always sold house lumber, while the Feldman's sold rough lumber, farm lumber and lumber to bridge contractors.

The only other lumber yard at this time in Lancaster was Garrard Lumber located at the present site of Sutton Pharmacy; Lucian Colson operated this lumber yard and built houses. Mr. Colson and Lewis Layton had operated a lumber yard just across the street from the present location of my sales office now. It too was called Garrard Lumber. Mr. Colson and Mr. Layton were excellent business men and we always got along well.

My first two years in business in Lancaster were almost a disaster. The years 1966-67 were good years for building, but I had inherited few customers. Some of Ross's old customers seemed to resent the fact that I had taken over. My business had gone down about twenty percent of his average over his last five years. In fact, it got so bad that I told my Dad that I had an offer of a good job in Covington, Georgia that I might take. He did not like this idea and stated that he could write off what little loss we might incur from profits on other business ventures.

We used Zora Oliver and his two sons, Gary and Norman, to remodel the sales office and some Cynthiana contractors to rework the lower shed. We were set up for sales, but we needed customers. We had to change the species of lumber we were buying to keep the business going. Ross had bought nothing but yellow pine in all dimensions. The local contractors were using utility grade Douglas fir lumber. This lumber was straighter than the lumber Ross used and cheaper. It was not as strong, but to vie, I had to stock the same lumber.

The third year that I was in business a local contractor, Billy Lane came to me and asked the price of lumber. I told him I would be competitive and give him terms of ninety days. This meant that he had ninety days to get the house built before he paid me. He used two excellent carpenters and managed a number of jobs himself. While he was able to do anything himself, he usually managed the job and hired sub-contractors. This was the first experience I had in success at the lumber yard. My sales started to pick up and in 1968, we showed a fair profit for the year.

Central Kentucky Supply, an aggressive company from Lexington, started coming into Lancaster and selling a number of houses. I had to keep my prices honest and in line or I would lose what business we had gained. There is no easy way where a company has it made. There is always competition. This is America.

The next move I made was in Danville. Two Garrard county men had developed Streamland Subdivision, along Bergin Road. Neal and Lewis May had developed this project that included nineteen hundred square feet homes with at least three bedrooms. All houses had to be brick veneer and meet their personal restrictions.

To get this business, I had to lower prices and hope that prices of my replacement lumber would not go up too much. I had just bought two trucks, two and one half ton Chevrolets from my father's garage in

Cynthiana and had Jim Cherry from Stanford put three phase hoists on them. With this equipment, we could deliver at least eight or ten loads a day.

My sales had jumped from two thousand a day to six thousand a day. Success looked like it was staring at me from around the corner. Sales beget sales! This is almost always true. A local lumber yard in Danville was angry with me because I had taken all of his business. I do not blame them at all, I know the feeling.

These Danville customers would buy three or four houses at one time. Coupled with the Lancaster business, things were moving better than planned. The May Brothers would use the best grade of white pine interior doors with clear casing installed. They would use half inch plywood for sub-floor and roof sheeting. While they would not use my drywall, they did use expensive walnut paneling and other high profit finish materials. Too, we sold shingles, base board, casing, crown molding, chair railing, and stair parts.

I would have to give a new quote on each house that these contractors would start. For a four or five year period I got most all of their business. I remember that Lewis May got very ill and passed away first. Neal May still would buy from me until he quit the business in about 1975.

With this success came more problems. When I took over the business, we had an accounts receivable of about twenty thousand dollars with an inventory of about the same amount. Too, we had about twenty thousand dollars in the bank with a debt of twenty thousand dollars.

At this time in 1974, we had sales of four hundred thousand dollars, compared to sales of only eighty thousand dollars in 1966. We had an inventory of one hundred thousand dollars, now compared to inventory of only twenty thousand dollars. Accounts receivable went straight up, but we had nothing in the bank, since we carried all customers ninety days or more.

Where does the money come from? I was fortunate in having my father, who was the President of the Farmers National Bank in Cynthiana. Too, I borrowed from the National Bank here in Lancaster. With the two of them, I was able to stabilize the sudden growth of the business. The only thing that a banker sees is how much you have in the bank! They will loan you all the money you want if you have a lot and do not really need the money. I needed about two hundred thousand dollars very badly. I do not think Willie Hugh felt that we were going to be a success after all. In fact I overheard him talking to a member of the board of the First National Bank in Stanford about my company. He did not know that I was in hearing range. I got enough of the conversation to realize that he felt that we might go under. While I did not interrupt the informal discussion, I did relay the information to my father that night by phone.

He came over the next day and asked Willie Hugh if he was happy with the forty thousand that we had borrowed from the National Bank here in town. Willie Hugh squirmed around in his seat and replied that some of the local people that I was selling had little net worth. They were not the richest people in town. However, if he would sign all of my notes, everything would be all right for now.

My father told him that if the local builders were people of wealth, they would not be building houses as contractors. The general contractor has to put up with problems that no one else can imagine. Few people have the aptitude to manage such an operation. When you finally get your money from the person that buys the house, they nit pick you to death. They think you got rich on the twenty thousand that they just paid you. Many seem to resent even giving the final payment to the poor contractor. I even feel that the contractor had a more difficult job than I have. Believe me I have been in his shoes and know some of what he goes through.

I guess my father lectured Willie Hugh for an hour or so and closed by stating that since our sales and inventory as well as account receivables had moved north, where in the world did he think the money would come from? It might take a year or so for the bank balance to catch up. All of the people we sold materials to were honorable. Again, all that the banker sees is your bank balance, and not the hard work.

Even after you collect your money from the outstanding jobs, more business will come your way if you are fortunate. At this time, we were. It seemed like we got every house that we bid. To make matters better, the Danville lumberyard that we took the most business from heralded the news that we were going broke!

At first I was mad at this slander. Too, I caught the owner of that particular lumber yard snooping in my inventory one evening. As I approached him he asked how we could sell so cheap. Was my grade of lumber as good as his? Was I selling inferior merchandise? The best way to handle this is to make him guess. I just told him that I had a buying advantage over him. That he would have to hunt sources of material that were new on the market. Then I told him that I would show him the rest of the lumber yard and that he was welcome at my business anytime. With this, he left a friend, not an enemy.

The biggest favor that he did for me was spread the news that we were going broke. Other contractors in Danville wanted to get in on the cheap lumber while the getting was good. I knew what they were thinking, "Take advantage of Bastin while there is still time." When some of the chain yards beat me in a deal, and they have plenty of times, I never say that they are going broke. Never! I just try harder. That is the American way.

Willie Hugh became the best friend and banker that our company had. Many times I would send checks to west coast lumber yards and it would take two weeks for the check to return to our bank in Lancaster. This gave me time to collect some of my money. Let me just say that the bank here allowed me to get by with murder many times, knowing that they could get their money from my father, if necessary. During this period, Mr. Sanders, Bob Guyn and Homer Profitt were just what the local lumber dealer needed. I was most fortunate to have these three bankers on my side during the 1970's. They made my business life much easier. If a new contact in the material business called the bank to find out about our credit, I always got the very best reports. Their testimony helped us so much and I have always appreciated it. Without that help in that particular area, no company can make it.

One time, Willie Hugh Sanders tried to help a little too much. He recommended me as worthy signer to an acquaintance that wanted to borrow money from the National Bank. This person, who both Willie Hugh and I knew, was from another city. Willie Hugh told him that the bank could not loan money to anyone who lived outside the county. The bank had to have a local signer. Knowing that this person might come to me, he pointed out that Hal Bastin's name would be fine.

The person called me with this request. I said no, that I had promised my family never to do this, as we had enough debt of our own. Oh, they declared, "you do not have to loan us the money, we will get it from Willie Hugh. You just have to sign." Still, I told them no. If they failed to pay, I would. I called Willie Hugh and he just laughed.

Through the year of 1974 we had increased our sales each year. This has to stop sometime. No one can keep selling more each year, especially when building recessions pop up. I call the 1970's the up and down years. There were many contrasts such as double digit inflation and recession; wage and price freezes along with rising unemployment. Also with record high housing prices that also dropped.

President Nixon, out of character, imposed wage and price freezes in 1971. The Arab Oil Embargo of October 1973 to March of 1974 twisted the world economy. This started an energy crisis as well as inflation and commenced a three year recession.

This caught up with my business in 1975. Our sales slipped by almost two hundred thousand dollars in one year. This short lived crisis focused attention on energy efficiency. It was much easier to sell insulation in the form of Tuff R board as well as fiberglass kraft faced R13. Now, contractors would insulate under floors as well as walls and ceilings.

The United States abandoned the ban on gold and allowed the dollar to float free on the international money market. Gold had been pegged at thirty-five dollars an ounce since the Great Depression and now would rise to a point over one hundred dollars an ounce in 1973 and reach five hundred eighty dollars by 1979. It would reach its apex briefly at nine hundred ninety dollars an ounce in 1980. Interest rates climbed and home mortgage rates went to over ten percent by 1979.

The first few years of the 1970's saw a boom in housing starts which peaked at over one million in 1972. This particular year was a great one for us in Lancaster. In 1975, the starts dropped to six hundred thousand. This was the lowest since 1946. By 1978, starts again topped the two million mark before falling the next year. The year of 1978 was our best to date at Bastin Lumber, when our sales topped at one million two hundred thousand dollars.

New federal government agencies were born out of this decade, and many new regulations were created. The EPA and OSHA placed pressure on the lumber businesses in many ways. Cheap western lumber from the United States was a thing of the past. Now, high interest rates and lumber shortages pushed by environmental restrictions changed the way material men did business. I personally think that these two agencies have done more damage to the country than good. They have destroyed our balance of trade with other nations. We have huge amounts of standing timber waiting to be harvested. By protecting the Spotted Owl, we encourage forest fires and poor conservation.

If we conserve our timber like the Greens want, then we deplete Canada. This is just as bad. Their land is right next to ours and will have the same effect. There is no rational thinking in allowing Canada to do what we won't. It just hurts our balance of trade and places a mountain of debt on our children.

Now, in 2006, much of our house framing lumber comes from Europe. Our automobiles come from Japan and framing lumber from Germany! You wonder who actually won World War II.

In the midst of our up and down ride, a deep depression came to the nation and our lumber yard starting in 1980, and for us it lasted through 1984. Most of the country rebounded by the middle of 1983. The year of 1984 was our worst year since the 1960's. During this period, I talked to a number of men about my age that lost their business during this recession. Many shared with me the fact that their grandfather took their lumber business through the Great Depression of 1929 and handed it over to their family during World War II. Perhaps a father took it into the 1960's and the grandson lost it in this recession of 1980. It was that bad.

The year 1982 brought the highest unemployment rate since 1940. Inflation dropped below four percent in 1982. In the country, housing build-up was at one million, the lowest since 1946. You did not want to sit on any spec houses at this time. It was almost impossible to sell.

At this time, a real blessing came from lumber heaven to our company. Miles Estates was created at the junction of Highway 52 and Old Danville Road. Several contractors from Nicholasville that I knew built most of them and this allowed us to show a profit in two years that would have been a disaster. For some reason, the next year, 1984, would be one of our worst.

In 1970, I bought a farm on Old Danville Road and added to it in 1978. All in all, I had about one hundred thirty-six acres and enjoyed working with cows. I always could get my lumber yard workers to help out in a pinch, when I had to cut calves or do something else to manage them. It is hard enough when you manage yourself and make sure nothing goes wrong. I have seen a lot of money lost by investors that did not look out for their farming interests.

During the last years of ownership in the Casey County boundary of timber that I have mentioned before, we made little or no money. An acquaintance of mine along Brush Creek tried to get me to go in halves with him on raising steers. He said that he would manage and fix fences and do all of the manual labor. I would furnish the grass and we would split 50-50. Too, he would put up half of the money to buy the steers. I had known his father well and trusted him. Still, I would not invest any money in something that I had little or no control over. People had stolen timber from us on this property and would actually steal the property itself if I had not made a land survey in 1966. I told this gentleman that I did not want to go into the cattle business with him.

I had been in the cattle business only a short time here in Garrard County and had done fair. Cattle were going up each week and you could probably run about one hundred head on the acreage. This was excellent snake land, but poor when it came to farming. This old friend called me again each month or so to see if I would change my mind. Each time I had to tell him "no".

It seemed that every week or so he would ask again, so I finally told him not to call again. I did not mean to be rude to him since he had done me favors about calling me if something went wrong on the land. I always needed a contact that I could reach if a problem came up on a gas line or something like that. Still, I was beginning to be put out with a call each month. I remember one night he called about midnight and I did not even allow him to get past a greeting on the phone. I said NO! I do not want to talk about it; I am not going to put anything on that snake infested property.

Finally, when I was out of breath, he said, "Hal, I just called to tell you that your seven bent barn had burned up." Apparently some boys had a party in it and set it on fire by accident. I had no insurance on it, and there was no tobacco in the barn. His last words were, "Hal, if you will just keep quite for a second, I will tell you about your barn."

In November of 1981, the national average mortgage rate hit a high of 15.6 percent. No one would build with rates this high. On top of this, the chain yards were expanding in Kentucky. Especially Lowes material branches would be the first to give me competition. They were first located in Lexington, then Danville. Later, Eighty-Four Lumber expanded in all the major cities around Lancaster.

During the 1980's we had more success in Nicholasville than anywhere outside of Garrard County. We were fortunate in selling to Donald Day and Mike Hopkins, who were the developers that got me interested in building duplexes. We built our first two duplexes in 1988.

The last five years of the 1980's brought improvement and records to our sales. Reagan's tax cuts paid off. Business was excellent and the future was promising. The years 1990 through 1993 brought a drop in lumber business and a slight recession. Housing build-up reached their lowest point in 1991. This was the lowest since 1946. Interest rates had finally dropped below ten percent. Inflation stayed on an even keel and housing build-up grew until 1995.

By 1996, a housing boom had started that would last to the end of the century. Most lumber yards that could stand off the chain yards would do well. While our business was hurt by the chains, we were in a county that had none.

From 1992 until 1997, I coached in the youth baseball league at the JC Baseball Park. This hurt my business greatly, and it was hard to recover. Still, 1997 through 1999 were banner years. The whole industry did well during these years. We had a Democratic executive with a Republican Congress. Perhaps divided leadership is not so bad.

During this time environmental issues continued to affect the industry. There was a long running situation with asbestos. The Johns Manville Company was broke because of this. From this time on, if a person bought property they had better make sure that there was no asbestos on it or an underground gas tank. They had better not sell paint with lead in it and remove any underground gas tanks that they might have.

Later, the arsenic was taken out of treated lumber for

precaution. Toxic mold was a new environmental issue that presented itself at the turn of the century. Health insurance and workers compensation insurance costs rose at an alarming rate during this time to make it more difficult on the local lumber dealer.

I inherited James I. 'Buddy' Johnson from my Uncle Ross Bastin. Buddy had been at the lumber yard since 1948. I was sorry that he only stayed a year or so after I took over the business. He was very quite and could do an exceptional amount of work for a small man.

The first foreman that I hired really made the company move was Parker Surber. Parker had worked on a farm and had done well, especially with cattle. I would probably admire this foreman as much as any man I ever came in contact with for the way he lived his life away from the business as much as he did in the business.

A good portion of his life was spent taking care of his wife who was an invalid for a long period of time. While many might have placed her in a nursing home, he stayed and took personal care of her. Too, he had lost a son, James, in about 1992. During these times, you never heard him complain. On top of this, he broke his neck while working at another lumber yard. When you watch a man go through difficulties like this with an excellent spirit, you wonder where he gets his inspiration. Parker testified that his came from the Lord. I certainly believed him.

A number of times when I went to the yard to work on a Sunday afternoon, he would be there on his own time straightening the lumber up to be ready for Monday morning. There was little foolishness about Parker Surber. Not many jokes, he was all business.

There was a family of Gilliam's that worked for me through the 1970's and into 1988. George was the first. He, as well as the rest of his family, had a wonderful disposition. When George injured his knee he had to retire. His brother, Albert took over. He was much like George and did a wonderful job. Vernon, another brother, was with us during this period as well.

After the Gilliam's left, a young man came in asking for a job and I could tell he was who I wanted as soon as I interviewed him. Some people just know how to work. Pat, "Speedy" Wall did. Speedy would be the kind of person that you would not mind sitting down or resting. He could do a complex job in minutes where it would take most men hours. He has been with our family since 1992 and is still the foreman. He is a master with the fork lift and can fix anything. I am sure he was born with this ability. He could frame a house and wire it. If he had the tools he could plumb it and whatever else that may be needed. One thing that I am so thankful for is that there have been few accidents at my place of business. My family prays each day for our employees and their safety. As fast as Speedy works, he has been accident free.

In fact, I remember only one accident in the forty-two years that I have been at the helm of this business. It happened in August of 1973. Garrard Lumber had closed down and I was fortunate in hiring one of their best employees. He was in his late 70's and skinny as a rail. He had plenty on money and did not need to work. If I had been him, I would have retired to Florida.

Willie Coulter could not retire or even think about Florida. He was happy working and would have been depressed if you told him he could not work. In those days, we received at least seventy or eighty cars of building material. As much as half of the lumber we ordered would come in via the L & N Railroad in a box car. The box car would be loaded so full that the first man would have to lay down in it to where he could touch the ceiling of the car. There was not much room for the first man to get into the car. Too, in summer the box car would be so hot that you could not touch the metal roof, which would be inches above your body.

Willie wanted this job of being the first to start unloading the box cars. He did an excellent job that a person half his age would be proud of doing. Fortunately, in a couple of years all lumber would arrive in a flat, gondola car that could be unloaded with just a fork lift. One man could do the job of five.

While being told not to hop on the fork lift while in motion, Willie enjoyed riding it while the foreman moved it about through the lumber yard. One August afternoon, I heard Lydia Montgomery, a clerk; shout that something terrible had happened! With a package of two by ten fourteen feet long on the lift, the driver negotiated a slight rise in the pavement with Willie hanging on the side. The lumber was at a height to where it was out of balance when he hit the rise and fell on Willie as he slipped to the ground.

When I arrived in seconds, I saw Willie under the package of two by tens. I immediately had Lydia call the ambulance and I rode with Willie to the hospital. He was bleeding, but could talk and seemed to have all of his vital signs. Fortunately, after a two week stay in the hospital, he was able to come back home. After he recovered, he wanted to come back to work in the worst way. I can not remember if he came back for a short while or not. As you might imagine, all of my contractors liked this excellent worker.

Considering the number of years that I have been in business, I have had few secretaries. When my Uncle Ross Bastin ran the business, he managed his own office, bookkeeping, and answered the phone himself.

Perhaps the best truck driver that has ever worked for our family I recruited in 1995. I drove out the Fall Lick Pike in the Fall of that year and talked to Gatewood Phillips into working for me. This was my lucky day. Gatewood had an engine that never stopped. If he wasn't delivering a load he was straightening out the lumberyard. This man could deliver more loads, faster and safer than anyone I know. Too, all of our customers liked this man.

I broke precedent with this policy within the first year of my tenure. My first secretary was Judy Maupin (Browning). She stayed about a year, which was not long enough for us to reach our first building boom. She did an excellent job.

My next secretary was Barbara Ray. She started in 1970 and stayed until 1978. She went through the roller-coaster years of the 1970's. She set up an excellent set of books and performed all the duties of a secretary, which included the easy side of collections as well as keeping books and helping me with sales. She was a very able worker and I was sad when had to resign after about ten years of work.

My next secretary was Patty Nunemaker and she stayed for fourteen to fifteen years. When you find a good employee, you do not want to see them leave since it is difficult to train another. You get used to their way of doing things and resent change. Patty caught on the building business quick. She was especially good in collecting accounts. While I have always been the one to collect the difficult accounts, I have always needed help in collecting the normal to slightly difficult accounts. Patty was excellent in this field as she was accurate with her bookkeeping. Too, she brought along her father, Jess Pollard, who at times would fill in for us when we were busy. I could get Jess only at odd times, since he did not need employment. He was the kind of worker that spoiled you and I often wished that I had been blessed with his abilities for the whole tenure of my business life. He was that good.

Patty saw the real ups and down of the lumber business. She saw us make money and saw the lean years and recessions where business was not so good. The years average out for most lumbermen and you must accept this business with that attitude. If you don't, you will be disappointed.

My current secretary is Kay Shuler. Not long after Kay started, I lost my brother who actually managed this business during the summer of 1951. Ross Bastin got very sick and had to have an operation that summer and was out for about two months. He was about twenty that year and did an outstanding job. Later that year he took a job in a Louisville bank before he had to go to the armed service and finally to Korea during the war.

After leaving the armed services he graduated from the University of Alabama and became a stock broker in Louisville. At one time, not long after my father died in 1977, he considered joining me in this business. He was an excellent business man and we would have managed well together.

Kay has now been with me seven years and is very popular with all of my customers. She is excellent with numbers and keeping records. She has an excellent disposition and is good at selling. If she has a fault, I have not found it yet.

I am thankful that I have had such good employees during my tenure. The reason that I almost left this section out of the book is because I have had such good employees and did not have space to mention all of them.

The century started out good for us and got better until this year, 2006. This has been a recession year in spite of reasonable interest rates. We were blessed with low rates for the last several years and customers expect them to be no higher than five percent. I hope they come back to that level soon. Too, across the nation, many houses stand unsold. When this supply is depleted, building will certainly go up.

Authors Hal and Kent Bastin

Kevin Bastin and Gatewood Phillips

Hal with mother Charlotte and father Hob in 1972

L to R-Hal Bastin, Patty Nunemaker, Albert Gilliam, and Frankie Day in 1983

Chapter 11

The Education of a Lumber Dealer

My personal education consisted of a BA degree from Eastern Kentucky University and three years in graduate school at Emory University. To be eligible to attend Eastern I had to graduate from an accredited high school. I attended my first three years at Kentucky Military Institute. I did not enjoy this school of strict discipline. It seemed that my bed was never made up quite right or I was out of line in some small thing. As soon as I caught on to a particular problem, the teacher had moved onto something I did not understand. While I loved their sports program I did not like the academics.

I attended the two week early football program in August of 1954. KMI did not have lights so we practiced twice a day in the August heat. I remember losing four or five pounds that I really didn't have to lose. The coach wore you out. You were not ready for any night activity after practicing with Coach Pace. Even if you felt like it, you could not leave the campus.

The regular students came back about the first of September and things returned to normal. The ranks of cadets came out and I was upset that I did not get much. I did something that I only tried once in my life and got by with it. I called my Dad in Cynthiana and told him to come and pick me up the next morning that I was disgusted with the military school after three years and wanted to come back to Cynthiana and graduate. At first, he objected, but when he saw that my resolve was at its peak, he relented.

About nine a.m. the next morning he pulled in the beautiful drive to the administrative building at their campus and picked me up. I threw my belongings in the1954 Chrysler and asked him to leave without notice. He did not cooperate with this line of thinking. He sought out Major Pace, the football coach and explained that I would be leaving. I did not hear their conversation, but in about ten minutes after the conversation my dad came to the car and we drove off with no begging me to stay.

I immediately sought out Coach Carl Genito in order to play football and be eligible for the next week's game. As I hoped, everything was all right. If I had been going from Cynthiana to KMI this late, I would not have been eligible to play, but coming back to my home town was no problem.

We had a fair season that year and won more games than we lost. I enjoyed playing at Cynthiana a lot and especially for Coach Genito. However, when it came to the academic part of school, I did not improve much. I had trouble with English IV under a Ms. Duffey. She was old and dull. By the end of the year it was almost sure that I would fail English and therefore fail the whole year. Hob to the rescue!

Hob was a personal friend to Mr. Cason the School Superintendent. Mr. Cason was a German and looked like a bull dog. Most people had some fear of him and for good reason. He did not put up with any monkey business. He demanded and got respect. Hob told him that it would do no good to keep me in that high school another year. Mr. Cason agreed.

But how could a deal work out where I would graduate and satisfy my English IV standards? My grade was perhaps at least five points below passing. Ms. Duffey had already declared that no one would get a chance at another test. All of this took place in early May of 1954. Finally, Mr. Cason promised that he would pass me if several others in the same boat I was in passed. My Father and I were both ecstatic. Ms. Duffey was also happy that she did not have to put up with me for another year. However, she was angry that I got through without meeting her minimum standards. She would not approve and dug her heels in and almost stopped the deal from becoming a fact accomplished.

With all of this going on, I almost ruined it myself. After a date one night, I met up with some of my friends and while driving around drinking some beer, we came upon Mr. Cason driving out the Millersburg Pike with his lady friend. WOW! This was an opportunity that we could not pass up, even if a deal was in place.

Bulldog Cason was not married and had every right to date whomever he wanted. The best I can remember, he had some lady named Adams in the car with him. We allowed them five or ten minutes or so to arrive at their parking spot at Jones' Shop. We were sure that we knew

259

where their destination was since we had observed this couple before.

Mr. Cason had a sharp, dark green 1954 Dodge automobile. It had an original dodge head ornament on the front of the hood that is a collector's item today. He always observed the speed limit and probably arrived about the time we allotted him. Perhaps in ten minutes or so we pulled just behind him in a 1949 Chevrolet Coop. I remember that my friend who was driving had the car in reverse in case Bulldog came out of his car in a bad humor.

After blowing on the horn and shouting "Bulldog, come up out of there" about five times we were ready to leave him alone. We saw no sign of this strict disciplinarian that night. All the time my friend had the car in reverse ready to go. I admit that with all the merriment there was an element of fear.

Since there was only one day left of school that spring, I told my parents that I would skip that day. I was assured of graduation and there was no sense in having to face Mr. Cason if it wasn't necessary. My parents would have none of it. About the only good thing that I had done all year was to be present at school every day and on time.

There was no other way around the problem. I would just tell my parents what we did the night before and they would understand that no one would want to face Bulldog Cason. Surely they would understand. I had already obtained a summer job and was on good terms with my parents for once.

I was surprised that my Father took it as well as he did. He never liked any monkey business, especially since Mr. Cason had been so nice to us. I told them that it was actually doing the school a favor by me and several others not having to attend the next year.

Dad said, "Not to worry!" He had talked to Mr. Cason only the night before at the Elks Club and declared that he was very sick. In fact, Mr. Cason was so sick he thought he might have to go to the hospital. Mr. Cason had told my Father that he would not be back to school until the graduation ceremonies and maybe not even then. Mr. Cason had some kind of flu and he was very weak. Dad said that Mr. Cason had to be helped down the steps and driven home by a friend.

While I did not want to go to school with this over my head, I relented when I saw that my parents would not bend. I drove my 1955 Chevrolet Bel Air hardtop up to the school and visited with my friends as usual that last day of school. I seemed to have a special spring in my step as I ran up the steps of the old Cynthiana School building for the last time. Just as I got to the main hallway I heard wham, wham, wham. WOW! Out of Mr. Cason's office came one of the school's worst butts. I do not know what he had done, but Mr. Cason was right behind him and mad! Mr. Cason did not look sick! I kept my head down and walked straight to my class. Somehow I don't think he saw me. I had seemed to get by with this one. Later in the day, I had asked my other party companions if Bulldog had said anything to them. Negative!

THE REVENGE OF BULLDOG

Three days had now passed and graduation day was at hand. I remember getting my cap and gown ready and driving up to school with my parents. I was warned not to pull off anymore pranks, and behave myself. I promised to be on my best behavior since nothing could go wrong now. Surely Bulldog did not realize that I was one of the sarcastic pranksters.

I remember assembling on the stage with our meager twenty-eight student graduating class. It would be one of the smallest in recent school history. Our graduation speaker was Dr. Frank Rose the President of Transylvania University in Lexington. The school was quite proud of the fact that we had such an esteemed speaker. As Mr. Cason introduced Dr. Rose, he pointed out all of the degrees Dr. Rose had earned and it was impressive, even to me.

At this time, I noticed that a man we called "Bear" Ward had entered the assembly hall dressed up in his best white suit. In fact, Bear Ward looked very much like Col. Harlan Sanders of Kentucky Fried Chicken fame. Bear attended all school functions even though he was somewhat eccentric. I was told years later that he played football at UK in about 1900. Bear could not hear very well and wore a huge hearing aid that took up what seemed like his whole ear. Hearing devices had not been perfected at this time and were rather large.

Bulldog was now ready for his revenge. Just before he turned the lecture over to Dr. Rose, he announced that the class would receive their diplomas in the rank of the grade point average. In other words, the valedictorian would receive his first, then the salutatorian and right on down the line in order of their grade point average. As this unique procedure started in progress it did not take me long to figure out that I would be dead last. As it got closer and closer to the twenty-eighth person, people started to giggle and poke fun at me. I have always been good natured and took it well. I certainly deserved their giggles. My parent's faces had already turned red with embarrassment. All other years the order of graduation was done in alphabetical order after the valedictorian. My mother knew since she had been a teacher for many years. Heck, I was glad just to get the certificate. It didn't bother me much. I would rather have this than a face to face confrontation with Bulldog Cason.

No sooner than the ceremonies and receiving of diplomas were given, Dr. Rose was called on to speak. I was rather interested in hearing what he might have to say since he had all of these degrees. I did not know it at the time, but several years later he would become the President of the University of Alabama. However, no sooner did Dr. Rose take over, he became tongue tied! I could not believe it. This man of letters could not think of a thing to say to this rather humble audience. His face turned red and then yellow. At first, I thought it was some kind of an act or demonstration, or perhaps some way to illustrate a great truth. The longer he went on struggling, people started to murmur and whisper. I was even starting to feel sorry for this great educator.

It seemed like an eternity, but about when everything was as bad as it could be in regard to his figuring out how to start, Bear Ward said "Louder". The whole place broke up. Bear thought that Dr. Rose was talking the whole time and his hearing aid was malfunctioning.

I was laughing so loud that tears were running down my cheeks. Fortunately for me, the rest of the class and many of the parents had broken up as well.

In a way, I felt that it served them right by trying to humiliate me and several others. I felt that at least I could get up there and give a simple speech.

I realized that I could not stay dumb for long. I wanted to go to college and study things that were of interest to me such as history, history, and more history.

I attended Eastern Kentucky University and graduated in 1959 with a degree in Social Studies. I took as much history as they offered, but found that school lacking in the subject that I loved most. While at Eastern, I had an experience that changed my life and probably insured my graduation as well as have me a purpose in life. At a revival meeting in Cynthiana, in 1956 I accepted Christ as my personal savior. This experience helped me in so many ways to actually find my way in life.

I spent three to four years in Atlanta, Georgia at Emory University studying Theology and Philosophy. While I considered going into the ministry, I came upon the opportunity to manage this lumber business in Lancaster, Kentucky. While in Atlanta I coached football and baseball and enjoyed the lifestyle.

In July of 1964, my Dad and I made the joint decision for me to start some kind of training in lumber business. As far as I knew, there were no schools that stressed just the lumber and building materials business. Also, I might have to go at any time to Lancaster since my Uncle, who was running the business at the time was old and might have to retire at anytime. Ross Bastin was eighty years old in 1965 and did an exceptional job in running this business at such a late age. However, his wife was very sick and it is anybody's guess how long a man that old could stay on top of a business.

My Father had sold his interest in Kentucky-Indiana Lumber Company in 1958 to his partner, Walter Freeman. Mr. Freeman had always been a friend of our family and had given my brother, Bob Bastin, a job several years before. While my brother appreciated this job a lot, his interest was in the stock brokerage business. By this time, he had been working with a concern in Louisville where he sold securities.

My Father called up Mr. Freeman and asked if he would give me a job, no matter how menial, for the length of time my uncle might need to finish his tenure in Lancaster. I am sure Mr. Freeman did not need a greenhorn that knew little to nothing about his business, but out of the goodness of his heart, he took me on. Hob and I did not care about how much I got paid so long as I was around lumber and building materials. I started off in July of 1964 and it was extremely hot and humid in Louisville on the Ohio River. I weighed one hundred ninety-five pounds when I started to work and by August I had lost down to one hundred seventy-five pounds. The foreman's name was Earl at this place of business. He pushed all employees and especially himself.

This work ethic seemed good for me but, I was not learning the business by just running a fork lift and picking up sash and doors. After a month or so, I told my Father that the Freeman's were very nice to me, but I wasn't learning too much. Some change had to take place for me to learn. They could not afford to give me a position of responsibility since I might leave at any time.

On Saturday afternoons, the only time we were off, I would go to any lumber yard that was open and try to find someone who might help me. I was always an outgoing person and had no trouble making friends. The only way you will get anywhere in this life is to go after what you want. I finally found a man who ran a lumber yard by the name of Camp Taylor Lumber Company, who was willing to help me. He actually pointed me to a certain Joe Johnson who worked for Weyerhaeuser Company in Louisville. I called up Mr. Johnson, a sales rep for that company for several years. He agreed to meet me each Tuesday night at a bar on Bardstown Road. I would buy the beer and he would answer any and all questions that I had.

While I did not drink myself, I footed the bill for his kindness in sharing this important information. You can find out about most anything if you are determined. While it took several weeks to find this source of information, it proved well worth it. Every Tuesday night we would meet and I would have the questions ready for him. What did he know about a small town lumber yard? Were the chain yards coming to Kentucky soon? Could independent lumber yards stand up to them? What was the quickest way to read a blueprint and spit it out into a contract? Who sold the best lumber and plywood at the lowest prices?

I suppose that he drank about seven or eight beers each sitting. He seemed to be able to drive home without any trouble. I know that if I had three beers I would need assistance in driving, I do not know how he did it. He was worth his weight in gold to my education. The whole time he was articulate until the seventh or eighth beer, so at that time I told him I had to go. No problem, same time next week.

It would be difficult to tell how much I have spent with Weyerhaeuser Company in the forty-one years I have been in business. Surely I have paid that company back for the Tuesday night education that Joe gave me. I hope Joe got his money's worth in this deal. Somehow, I don't think so. He stayed on at Weyerhaeuser for several years after helping me so much. I think he retired in about 1973.

I would look at as many profit and loss statements from lumber yards as I could find. I would keep this information confidential. If someone would help me, I would always treat them with respect. I had changed from my high school days. Too, I would buy sets of house plans and figure houses at an imaginary cost. Then I would take the results to my Father in Cynthiana on the next visit and see what he thought. His criticism was most helpful. While my Dad was an excellent businessman and Father, he was not a real good teacher. By this time, he was seventy-two years old and due a little rest from business. My Mother would not permit much business to pass his way. She took good care of him and tried to get him to avoid business problems before they started.

If a person wanted to enter this field now, in 2006, I would advise attending a school like Michigan State which has an excellent program for this line of work. There are several other colleges that offer a major in this field.

During my tenure at Bastin Lumber Company I have attended seminars almost every year in regard to products, freight, and collecting, selling and other phases of this business. They have been most helpful. I would never think that I have arrived and reached the point of not needing knowledge. My attitude has changed one hundred percent from the day I graduated from Cynthiana High School.

Hal Bastin with 1953 Ford

Chapter 12

Collections

Perhaps the most difficult job that one would ever have in any business is collections. If you sell on credit, this will be a major part of your work. Our business is no exception. We have had about every trick used on us to avoid or slow down the payment of an account.

My teacher was the best! His name was Lewis L. Walker. He was born in 1873 and died in 1944 during the Anglo-American invasion of Normandy amid the Second World War. Actually, he taught my father and my father taught me. He taught Hob to file liens, read deeds, business law and many things a practical business education would include.

Of course, I never met Lewis Walker. My Dad used him as a mentor. I appreciate the kindness he showed my father who did not have the money to attend college. This knowledge came in handy when a merchant attempted to collect his accounts.

In fact, I have always had a good friend that was a lawyer. I recommend this to anyone in business. This ability and knowledge will be needed. Know that for sure. Always try to stay out of court if possible. However, if necessary, be ready.

John E. Smith came to Lancaster the same year I did in 1965. I met him coaching little league football in 1966. He was with the firm of Cox and Eagle and seemed to know a lot about collection law. He always was very reasonable in his charges and in turn, I always tried to get him business. I probably came out ahead since when we coached or played golf I would run the days business by him and get his feedback.

My Dad always said that if we could collect ninety-eight percent of our credit accounts, we could stay in business. Below that line and you were in trouble. Above it, and you did very well. I have stayed at about ninety-nine percent of my credit accounts which seems fine, except when you see that we have sold sixty million dollars or so that comes up to fifty-five thousand dollars. I have lost at least that much down through the years. True, the IRS is very fair in allowing you to write this off, but, you still hate to lose it.

The above amount seems like a lot to sell, but, in this case it is a small lumber yard. The margin of profit is not like a hardware business or a drug store. We get to keep only a small portion of our sales. Many customers pay us a check of twenty thousand dollars for their lumber on a house. Many of them think we are getting rich when they give us their check. They do not realize that we have to pay for gas, salaries, electric bills and so forth. Our gross margin of profit is only about twenty-two to twenty-three percent.

I have had customers tell my secretary when they pay, "Well, if Hal needs the money this bad, here it is." That comes after five collection letters and a threat to small claims court. You cannot believe some of the excuses not to pay. Many years ago, it was "Wait until I sell my crop." I have not heard that particular excuse in a long time.

My banker is on vacation and as soon as he gets back I will pay you. This is a good one. In other words, this person does not have enough responsibility to find out just when his loan officer is going on vacation. Only a little foresight would have solved this problem.

Fortunately, the State of Kentucky has had good lien laws throughout most of my tenure in business. The laws in 1966 to 1975 were excellent. From 1976 to the late 1980's they were changed to favor the consumer. Since that time, they have been much improved.

Basically, they state that if a contractor builds a house for a third party, the lumber yard has up to six months after the last day materials were delivered to file a lien. This means the property cannot be sold unless the lumber dealer is paid. He might not get interest or delivery charges. But, he should get his basic account. Usually, this is all the lumber dealer wants. Just get out of the mess.

I have filed many liens myself in Garrard and all of the counties that surround us. However, if an account is over twenty thousand dollars, I usually get a lawyer. In one case, about eight years ago, Mark Metcalf saved me about twenty-eight thousand dollars! The people did not have enough money to pay all accounts after getting all they could from their bank. Their financial institution would give them no more money. I am quite sure that they misspent some of the funds. This happens much of the time when there is not enough money left to pay all accounts.

Too, they were getting a divorce! I did not know who would pay what with what! Mark made them, while they were in a good mood, sign a second mortgage and a note to me. It was lucky that he caught them before they refused to speak to each other. Too, he placed a builder's lien on the property. They allowed a real estate company to sell the property. It brought more than appraised so I came out well. You need a lawyer! I never saw two people more mad than when they saw how little were going to be left over after the dust settled. Poor Mark got an ear full. He told me that he was use to it.

The worst case that we ever faced came in Jessamine County. There was a contractor that was building several houses and paid well. Then, he builds a four bedroom on speculation. After paying a small first installment of about four thousand dollars, he failed to pay anymore. The house was finished and his carrying period was up, but I could not find him. He had taken his last draw, bought a pick up truck and left the state. We did all we could to find him, but to no avail. Naturally, we placed a lien on the house. It sold at a Master-Commissioners sale and failed to bring enough to pay us. In that case, I just lost! That was my largest loss for just one house.

Now, if you look at the case in its whole, I did profit on the several houses that he did pay me for. I did collect some of the money due me on this one. I got to write off my loss on this account. So, all in all, this deal did not go so bad. However, you cannot take many of these cases. You won't be in business very long.

At the same time, we were in a class action suite over twenty-five railroad cars of plywood. It seemed like Weyerhaeuser, Georgia Pacific and some of the other large manufacturer's plywood had charged lumber yards too much. We received a check from the class action suite of about as much as we lost in the above case. I felt that someone up there was watching after me. In fact, I have felt that I have been in God's will all the years I have been in Lancaster. While bad things happen some of the time, He will forgive and pick you up and guide your life. As I look back through the years, I can see how he has guided me and realize a pattern in my life. It is much more difficult to look out in the future and see it. However, as I look back I can see His hand.

The next trick that my Dad taught me to watch out for is the double check trick. Say a shady customer owes you money and you owe him some. This happens lots of times in this business. He always owes you much more than you owe him. After many efforts to collect, you finally catch him and he suggests that you all exchange checks. Beware of this! Make sure his check goes through before you give him your good check. He is slick and will go and cash yours before you realize his bounces.

It is always best to check the lending institution when a person sets up an account. Make sure they promise to take care of the lumber portion of the account. People will take advantage of your kindness and patience. While this does not always work, usually lending institutions will honor a commitment. However, there is so much competition in this business that many lumber dealers are so glad to get a house that they fail to check up and do their homework.

Not long ago, we had an account where the lending institution told us everything was fine. In a couple of months, when the account was due, they changed their mind and decided not to back the house. I did not get their commitment in writing and this was a mistake. They let the clerk go that made the commitment. I am not sure exactly why, but, I could guess.

I placed a lien on the property and this seemed to protect us from a disaster. Fortunately, the people who were building the house had the lot paid for. Without the equity in the lot, I might never have been paid.

From day one, everything went wrong. The house was not quite under roof. Perhaps ninety percent of the roof sheeting was on and that was covered only with fifteen pound felt black paper. When the bank decided to cut all payments on this house, it could not come at a worse time. The material supplier does not want to give enough material to get it under roof and safe from weather while lawyers pan everything out. The contractor will not donate his time to finish the roof even if materials were furnished. The job is at a stand still at the worst time.

The customer does not have the money to just get it under roof. It sits in the rain and sun until it can be auctioned. Only then if all agree. Even when this happened, it took seven more months to get it ready for auction. The one good thing was the beautiful fall day it was auctioned off. While only a small crowd attended, there were several potential buyers that bid it up to where all would be paid. Everyone breathed a sigh of relief when the auctioneer's mallet banged down for the last time and he declared SOLD! I immediately called up the contractors and told them the good news. We only had to wait one month and everything would be fine.

The lucky buyer even forked up a substantial deposit to where we were leaving all worries about this account and thinking of other accounts to worry about. One month passed and no money! Two months passed and we found that the buyer could not get a loan. Can you imagine buying a beautiful piece of property like this and no preparation for payment? For some reason, banks would not loan money on this account. Perhaps because of the large amount it would take to finish the house. Since it had ten foot ceilings and many square feet to complete, banks were skeptical of it. Interest rates were at reasonable level when this experience happened, so we wanted it sold before they might go up.

After three months, the whole thing fell through. To make matters worse, the customer took bankruptcy. Now, even to sell the house, we must get it out of bankruptcy and find someone who might want to buy the house. The house was a deteriorating commodity. While still and excellent value, each day of sun, snow, rain and wind did the structure no good.

Can you imagine? Here is some odd sixty thousand dollars that you seem to almost have in your hand and it slips away. Imagine the feeling of going to bed one night thinking it is all right and the next night realizing it is a long way off, if ever. In this case, several times I just prayed that I would take one day at a time. If I lost it, so be it! My family was healthy and in good spirits and we had plenty to eat and a nice house to live in. Be happy with what you have!

On the other hand, it makes you look stupid and incompetent as a businessman to allow something like this to go through your business. Was it planned out? Was there a design behind the trouble? I was sure not! Still, there were more things to go wrong with this collection than any I had ever had to collect.

Finally, a contractor said that he could pay me and the other debts off and take the house. Again, he was financially able to do what he said he would do. No problem there. Again, everything seemed ready to go. Then, something happened to this contractor. Again, we were back to square one. If you can stand this type of experience you can make it in the lumber business. While not an every year occurrence, it can happen. Your emotions go up and you are elated and then go down when things do not fit.

Several months later, a customer came along who saw the potential in this property. Rates had gone up marginally, but he had the resources and desire to purchase the property. Still, it took several months to finalize the deal. I do not think that I could go through an ordeal like this one again. I intend to stay in this business until my family won't put up with me. Perhaps after three generations at the same place, in the same business, it is hard to let go. I love it!

Once about twenty years ago, a man built an expensive shed or garage. I am not sure which you would call it. The account amounted to about fifteen thousand dollars including taxes. He pad it down to three thousand dollars and would pay no more. We placed a lien on it and waited. I have twelve months to perfect a lien for a judgment or I lose the lien. As usual, I watched my calendar and got my judgment. We still had no money. Five years passed. Finally, after I forgot about the account, he came in and paid fifteen hundred dollars on the account. He told me that he wanted the lien cleared off of his account and property. I told him that I would oblige him if this happened. Yet again, several years past, then, out of the blue, he came in again and declared he would pay five hundred more on the account. I told him that I only wanted the principal and would charge him no interest. While he seemed happy with that, he has never been back. The lien still stands as a cloud on his property. Who knows, he might be in sometime and pay it off.

Somewhere in the mid 1990's, we had a carpenter come to us and start two duplexes. It was in a near by town of which I will not name. This contractor usually did not have material charged to his account, but would charge the material to his customer. He had probably given my business twenty houses over a period of six or seven years. His customers paid on time and bought everything from me that I sold. Not just lumber and mill work. I was happy to see this carpenter come to see me with a house to figure.

I was able to get a reasonable mark up in a day that the chain yards made that difficult. He liked to use us because we would give good terms and his customers liked the way my secretaries kept the accounts. Customers were able to read the accounts even if they were not versed in building material nomenclature. In fact, he used several customers over and over. Too, they were happy with the fact that we would take back any extra material. They seemed to like the fact that they knew who to come to if something went wrong. I was very accessible. Unlike the chain yards, no one had to call district headquarters to see if a credit could be given. We had a good working relationship. I would figure the houses, send the materials and come to the job site to figure windows and doors and trim.

Nothing that good lasts forever. I found this out many times in this business. A customer this good is like money in the bank. Success spoils many men that have their first taste of prosperity. I began to smell liquor on his breath. Not long after that, he had his employees do most of the framing. I could tell that this situation would not last much longer.

After I talked with him, he seemed to perk up and become his old self again. He started the two duplexes and I let my guard down. Most of the time rental property pays well. Not this time. He took draw money and went south halfway through the project. Rates went up at this time and finally a master commissioner sale took place. While I filed my usual lien, too much had been drawn on this project for me to be covered. Fortunately, I lost only fourteen thousand dollars, since the jobs were in their infancy. Since I was charging to him, I had a large mark up and our loss was not that bad. However, any loss is bad and should be prevented. I just was asleep at the wheel!

This is not the end of the story. Two or three years later, this contractor came back to Kentucky and was able to talk one of his old customers into building a large house for speculation. He came to me for credit since he could go nowhere else. I did not lecture him on how he mistreated me or the wicked act he carried out in the past. Since it would be charged to his customer, I gladly accepted him and again made money. Never cut off your nose to spite your face. Control your ego. On the other hand, I will never credit him again. By the way, he did ask later.

There are many other stories that I could tell about collections. Fortunately, I have never gotten into trouble in a dangerous way in my collections. I feel that someone up there has watched over me in a special way. Anyone who has gone to homes, sent letters and called on the phone as much as I have in regard to the subject of money owed, could expect trouble. If you are afraid of that then you need not be in this business. Afraid perhaps, but you must go on anyway. You must do all you can within the law to collect on all accounts.

The closest to trouble was when I called a man about his account several times and then went to his house. His car was there, but he would not answer the phone. He came to the door when I rang the door bell and invited me inside. I was a little surprised at this. After presenting him with the bill in person, he exploded. I do not know if it was fake or sincere. He sure scared me in any case. I merely told him that I was now going to the court house and file a lien. As I made my way to the door he stopped me and began to talk reasonable. I had to take a car and a piece of property in on the account, but we got it paid.

I have always used Proverbs 15:1 as the basis of all of my collections. Believe me, it works with prayer. When I see the person is irrational, I stop and find an exit. There is not enough room for profit in this business to allow a collector to forgather your accounts. In fact, the best business manual that I have ever read is the book of Proverbs in the Old Testament. It has a gold mine of wisdom that few people bother to read.

Exactly how much stealing has gone on at my lumber yard would be hard to tell. I have had people come to me and confess that they took material and wanted forgiveness. This made me happy to forgive them since my sins will be forgiven in measure the way I forgive others. Too, I have many more come to me and point out others that have stolen from me. They always make me promise not to use their name. Therefore, I can rarely confront the accused thief since there is no way to back it up. All business has this.

Fortunately, most of our customers are good, decent working individuals. I have enjoyed working with them and seldom charge interest on their account. They have made the journey worthwhile.

This final story does not actually fit the pattern of a collection of the lumber yard. However, it could have developed into a major problem of my family getting ripped off. At least twelve couples in this scam were ripped off and for a lot of money.

I recall that this happened in February of 1988, the year Bush forty-one was campaigning for president in New Hampshire. About a month before, I received the letter in the mail inviting my wife and me to the conference on purchasing silver to be held in San Diego, California. Neither one of us had ever visited California, and it seemed too good to be true.

The Conservative Times, a right of center magazine, promised to send my wife and me to that beautiful west coast city free of charge if we would promise to be present at all of their lectures for five days. The lectures would start at 9 a.m. sharp and go until noon. After lunch, the afternoon would be free. You could go to the beach or shopping or to the zoo. We did all three.

They would have supper at seven p.m. sharp and an evening lecture that would last until ten p.m. The only thing we had to commit on was faithful attendance at each lecture. Too, you had to bring your wife. There were no exceptions. Since the wife must be in on any major business deal, the hosts wanted to make sure that both partners were present.

They made no bones about the fact that they wanted to sell you bars of silver as an investment. In order to get a free plane ticket and three free meals a day plus lodging at the LaJolla Marriot Hotel, you had to present your financial statement and a letter of credit from a national bank or authorized lending institution.

It took several hours of planning and preparation to meet their conditions. Too, I had to get my wife to promise to attend the lectures and stay awake. I had no idea what they might lecture on. Since the magazine was conservative and leaning toward Republican Party issues, I felt that it would not be too bad.

After they promised to accept my wife and I, and sent a brochure to describe our itinerary, it was my turn to ask questions. Would they use high pressure tactics to induce us to buy their product? Would they demand that we must promise to buy their silver bars in order to get the free trip? People never give something for nothing,

They had already looked at my financial statement and gleaned from it that I did not have a position in gold or silver coins. They could see from my portfolio that I was not a gold bug.

They made it clear that they advocated one should buy silver to protect against the anticipated collapse of our currency. They made the usual arguments that our country was now a welfare state and that it was a matter of time before inflation depleted our cash equivalents, stocks and bonds and even land. While I agreed with this philosophy over time, I was not sure if I wanted to buy from them and if so, maybe not now.

Actually, I feel that this country should be on a gold standard. Ever since the days of William McKinley and William Jennings Bryan, I felt that this country made a mistake by failing to go on a disciplined gold standard. That way, the politicians could not lie and promise the moon every election.

My party, the Republicans, who were supposed to be financially responsible, have come to office and spent like a drunken sailor several times. While the Democrats are much worse, neither party has a record of truth. Now, in 2006, the Democrats are the party that wants to control spending. Bless their hearts!

The only thing that will save the country is a line item veto. We will not get this. The Republicans ask for it but realize that the Democrats will not allow it. The Republicans are happy they won't.

Trust me! It will take a complete collapse of the currency for us to even think of a gold standard. Neither party wants financial discipline. This would stop wild promises that get them elected.

While I agreed with the general philosophy of this exciting conference, I felt that the time to buy gold or silver was not in 1988. Remember, if you buy their product, all it does is sit there. Too, you must put it in a bank or safe storage.

In mid February of 1988 Tensia and I boarded our Delta Aircraft and flew to San Diego via St. Louis. We arrived about four in the afternoon west coast time. A limousine was waiting at the airport to usher us to our luxurious hotel. While we shared this lavish transportation with another couple, it seemed silly to me to waste this resource. We could have hailed a cab as easy and we would have been just as happy.

I made the gentleman who arranged our itinerary promise to not use pressure tactics or arm twisting in their presentation. Dutifully, they promised to only present their case for silver and let the cards fall where they may. We just had to bring our spouse and attend the seminars. The reason for bringing your spouse was to eliminate the excuse of having to confer with her before you could make a decision. They wanted to eliminate any excuse. They had thought of everything you might object to.

The reason for your financial statement was to insure the fact that you had the propensity to purchase their product. Again, they eliminated any possible excuses that you might have. I could see this when I examined their program. I wanted to know how they would make enough money off of my wife and me to pay for this trip.

When we arrived at the hotel, we were surprised at the amenities that were offered. While we had to eat lunch and supper with the group, we had four different restaurants we could catch breakfast. Two of the days we were there we had a choice of these restaurants for lunch and supper. At that time the cost of just supper at one of these places would be about ninety dollars or so.

The banquets for lunch and supper with the group were even better with greater selection than the opulent restaurants in the hotel. My wife usually stops me from desert if I eat too much at the main meal. Not this time! I fully intended to take advantage of this set up. The food was there and would be wasted if it wasn't consumed.

To make matters even better, the roster of lectures promised to be excellent. First, a hotel owner from Germany would lecture on the inflation of the German Mark after the First World War. The Germans did this to pay off their war debts. They were smarter than the French or the British. However, it got so bad that in order to buy a loaf of bread in 1923, one had to have a wheel barrow to carry enough money. This German pointed out that he felt that inflation like this would come soon to America.

The next day they had a former American flyer that had been a POW lecture on the possible Americans that may still be in Vietnam. Perhaps he was the best on the itinerary. He told of the hardships that he went through for the good of our country. He was in the Hanoi Hilton prison camp for at least three years.

Most of the rest of the lectures were on runaway spending and broken financial promises of our government. Too, there were several lectures on the bankruptcy of Marxism and Communism. The Soviet

Union was still intact at this time. Several of the speakers would castigate the do good liberals of this country and their representatives in congress.

Finally, on Saturday at lunch we had attended the last lecture. After we had adjourned and were waiting for lunch to be served each couple was required to meet with a counselor for them to have a shot at selling their product.

My wife and I were patient with out advisor and listened to all of his arguments at buying at least twenty thousand dollars worth of silver bars. We explained that we would think about it and give an answer in a couple of weeks. We could not say that we did not have the money since they had our financial statement. I could not say I had to ask my wife, since she was there. This particular gentleman went through the sales pitch with class. I was afraid that any minute he might try to arm twist. While he came close at times, he veered away at the last moment. This was the most uncomfortable position we were placed in up to this time. I only had to remind him once that I would sift through his arguments and sleep on it for about a week. Finally, he agreed that he was finished and hoped that we had an enjoyable trip and experience. We assured him that everything was much above the way we were used to eating and living. There was no room for improvement. We thanked him again and left for the last lunch with the group.

While waiting on lunch to be served, we noticed that we had to wait a little longer than usual. Tensia took this opportunity to go to the ladies room and I sat in the lobby.

No sooner than she had left a well dressed young man came up to me and sat down with no introduction. He immediately scolded me for not buying at least twenty thousand dollars worth of silver bars. He pointed out that his price on silver was about the same as the current commodity price, he would offer financial information with an eight hundred phone number. I could call at any time, day or night, and get current quotes on stocks, bonds or prices on hard metals.

He asked if my wife and I were treated nice. Did we enjoy the food? Were the accommodations suitable? How was the plane ride from Kentucky? Again, with this salesman, I was patient. I actually felt a little guilty by accepting all of this free. Still, I allowed him to go around one time before I stood up to him.

He pointed out that with my portfolio I might be broke soon if I didn't have a position in hard metal. Didn't I agree with all of the lectures? What had they done wrong? Didn't I appreciate the hospitality? Now, it was difficult for me to get a word in edgewise.

I thought that they might kick my wife and me out of the hotel and tell us to find our own way back to Lancaster. The man was now close to obnoxious. I reminded him that he had broken his promise about high pressure. If I could not trust him in this, how could I trust his company with my cash? With this argument, my wife arrived and joined our conversation. For some reason, he immediately left us and started on another couple.

Lunch was served and we had the rest of the day free. We went to the beautiful San Diego Zoo. On the way my wife brought up the conversation she had with a doctor's wife she had met at the conference. It seemed like the doctor was formally a Cuban exile that had settled in St. Louis not long after Castro had come to power in Cuba. Tensia felt at home with this Spanish speaking lady and they swapped stories of their experience in America. Too, they wondered how the company that treated us to this wonderful week could make enough money to justify such an offering. I remember their names were Garcia and he was a foot doctor. They were very nice people.

After a wonderful day at the world's largest zoo located on one hundred acres of landscaped botanical gardens which was home to one thousand species of animals, we arrived back at our hotel for supper. Our meetings were over and we had no more pressure to buy silver.

The next morning a limousine picked us up and took us to the airport for our trip back home. It was a wonderful week especially since it cost us little to nothing. I still could not figure out just how this organization could pay for about ninety couples to enjoy themselves so much just on commissions on twenty thousand dollars worth of silver. The commissions are not that high. Their price was just slightly above what I could buy on the market at that time.

We arrived home on a Sunday afternoon and I made up my mind

not to fool with these people at any cost. There was no way they could make enough money on me even if I bought the twenty thousand dollars worth of silver.

The next week, they called my secretary every day trying to get in touch with me. They were told every time not to call again. If I was interested, I would call them.

After a month went by, I remember that I came in from feeding cattle on a Sunday afternoon and my wife asked me if I had bought any of this company's silver. I told her no, I had definitely decided against it for two reasons. First, I was not interested in buying silver at this time. Second, I did not trust this company since the figures did not add up. They could not make a profit on us.

She said that her friend, Mrs. Garcia, had just called from St Louis and was angry that this company would not send them their silver. They had given the company twenty thousand dollars but nothing in return. We were warned not to buy anything from this company. They were calling their lawyers in hopes of getting some of their money back.

Now it dawned on us how this company would fund the extravagant week they gave us. If six or seven couples would give them twenty thousand dollars each, they could make a good profit. While this story is not exactly a collection story, it could have been if we had purchased the silver. I feel sure that the doctor did not recover any of his money.

Chapter 13

Special Products

The first product that comes to mind is Perry-Derrick Paint. We started selling this paint in the 1930's and still have several cans on display from that era. Bob Goff and Ross Bastin actually sold more of this paint than I have.

In 1966, my first year, stores started mixing paint so they would not have to carry so much inventory. They just stocked a neutral white and had the mixes to make most any color that someone would like. Ross did not have such a mixer and I did not know enough about colors to buy one.

We have stayed with paint since 1966, but, carry only a few colors. Perry Derrick went out of business about 1999, so we changed to Gray Seal. It is as good as Perry Derrick, but we have a small volume.

The product that we have carried that has changed brands more than any other is shingles. Since my uncle's retirement, we have carried at least six brands of shingles. Atlas, Georgia Pacific and GAF are some of the name brands we have stocked.

We were not happy with any of these for long. Since the turn of the century, we have been very happy with Owens Corning brand. Too, most customers want the heavy, thirty year dimensional designer shingles. Since oil products have gone up so much, shingles have followed suit. My uncle sold shingles for six dollars a square. Now, I sell the designer shingles for about fifty dollars a square. Too, they are a much better product. His shingles were not even seal down. Seal down came in about 1965.

The next product is a designer product that is exceptional quality. I have always tried to persuade customers to use Andersen windows over any other. They are that good. We usually sell about three vans of this top quality product every year. In the last few years, we have slowed down from this quantity.

One of the first houses that I got in my first year was the Christian Church parsonage. The contractor called for Andersen windows. I was familiar with them since Weyerhaeuser jobbed them at that time. They had just discontinued their line of single glazed windows and now featured a welded glass window. This may have been the best window ever built. The frame and sash were wood and the jam was vinyl clad. At this time, they only offered white. They pointed out that you could paint it, but, I must admit that they did poor with paints.

Still, Andersen was a superior product to all other offerings at that time. They had variety of sizes and featured the very best in insulating value at that time. They offered awning, casement and double hung windows that could be mulled together to make most any combination. Their sales people were very helpful and catalogs were informative. They were expensive, but worth paying the extra cost.

In 1985, I started to buy these windows by the van load. This was a cost of about forty thousand dollars each time a van rolled into

Lancaster. A big investment! However, you got an excellent discount when you bought this way. We were able to compete with this product and actually take sales away from the aluminum window business.

For example, if a person purchased an Andersen, double hung thirty-two by twenty-four window from me in 1985; the chances would be excellent that they would have that same window today. They will last forever. The cost would have been about eighty-five dollars. If they bought the aluminum, insulated glass window, the cost would have been about forty dollars. The cheaper window would have to be replaced in about ten years. Which is the best buy?

Andersen was good in the marketing department. We put on special dinners at the Country Diner and White Barn for our customers. Andersen would pay half and I would pay half. Patty Nunemaker was especially helpful in arranging these meetings. Sometimes we would have as many as fifty people to attend one of these dinners. They would point out any new product that might come up in the near future. They were slow to go to a tilt window that the customer could wash. Finally, in the early 1990's they came out with a tilt/wash window that was energy efficient.

In 1988, Andersen came out with new product that would really catch on in windows. It was Low E glass. This glass could not be manufactured as the welded glass. The welded glass was actually only one piece of glass that wrapped around at the weather strip. They never fogged up and provided excellent insulation.

This new window, had argon gas fused between the panes as well as the tint that reflected sunlight out in summer and allowed it in during the winter when the rays were at a lower angle. Now, all window manufactures try to follow what the Andersen Company started.

Andersen would be the first to create a new, neutral color called sand tone. After twenty years their patent ran out so others could imitate. We still feel that Andersen is the best quality product in its field. I feel that it is the most inexpensive window that you can buy in the long run. It is a quality product.

If a person is bound to buy a vinyl window, I would council MW. This company has sold me building products for over thirty-five years. Vinyl windows appeared on the market in about 1983. They were much better than aluminum, since they were neutral when it came to heat efficiency. Vinyl is not as good as wood, which is a great natural insulator, but better than aluminum which is anti-insulation. Feel metal in cold weather and you will see what I mean.

MW has anything the customer wants in extras on windows. They will include J channel, jamb extenders, Low E glass with Argon gas, grills between the glass, and many other extras that the customer might want. They have single hung and double hung models that are attractive in price. Too, they have several colors to choose from. I have enjoyed my relationship with this company because of their excellent products.

MW offers awning, casement and single hung and double hung units that tilt for easy maintenance. They will pre-assemble quarter and half found units to make most any ensemble that a customer might want.

This versatile company even offers a period all wood windows with individual panes of glass that has fixed muttons. This is the only company that I know of that offers this series of window that is not special made. While I do not recommend this to the average customer, it is just what the person who builds a period home might want. While it would demand up keep, it is original. It would set off an early American home that would embrace the Williamsburg style.

In hardware, we have always stocked the Weiser locks. This product is not cheap, but it is one of the best quality door locks you can purchase. I put them in all of our family's duplexes and they are very durable. They do not ware out and are very attractive.

The last company that I would like to brag on is the Weyerhaeuser Company. I have mentioned the help one of their employees gave me when I first started out in this business. All of their salesmen have been equally as helpful. My secretary will vouch for their honesty in warning us when prices are about to go up or down. There are few salesmen that I would trust with this advice.

We have seen prices spike to extremely high levels, stay there for a few months, and then drop just as fast. A person could make a bundle or drop all of their profit in a short period of time. One can imagine how helpful that some sound advice from a truthful source might be in this kind of situation.

Their lumber and related products are of the best quality. Most of the time, we will buy our lumber from Weyerhaeuser even if the price is a little high. It is that much better. Too, we have other sources, but we love this Louisville based company. We have done business with them for forty-two years.

In the mid 1990's, laminated veneer lumber was offered and demanded by local building codes. This was another quality product that made houses stronger and safer. Weyerhaeuser carries an excellent line and has twice a week delivery service.

If a customer wants uniform widths in his floor joist, we stock Canadian I joist in many lengths. These are less expensive than Weyerhaeuser's product, but good quality.

Most of our customers still use traditional two by ten and two by twelve floor joist out of number two grade yellow pine. This lumber has to be grade marked, since all of the counties where we sell lumber have a building code.

When I first got in business in 1966, there was one company that stood out as a top supplier to lumber yards. It was the Combs Company in Lexington. The sold all kinds of millwork, sash and doors, and moldings. At one time, they even were a distributor for Andersen windows. One family had run this business for about a century. I was sad when this company went out of business.

My last story about products will center on a misunderstanding about the Andersen name. When I first started selling windows, I found out that there were two companies with the same name. One spelled it Andersen which had its offices in Bayport, Minnesota. This is the company that I used and have spoken of so highly. The other company was spelled Anderson and was based in Owensboro, Kentucky.

Many times people would come in and compare prices and wonder why my Andersen windows were priced so high. My answer was that it was the top of the line window. No! They would reply. I am pricing Anderson against you.... It didn't take me long to figure out why. It was not the same quality window. It was not vinyl clad like the Andersen I marketed. At some point in the 1980's this company sold out to a large manufacturer. Then, when they wanted to start back into production a few years later, they could not use the Andersen name. I think that the company I bought from, Andersen bought out the title to their spelling. While this made in Kentucky window was a fair product, it did not compare with the national brand, Andersen. I was glad that I did not have to go over the difference in the windows again.

About four years ago, a customer came to me requesting a top of the line window. I immediately suggested Andersen. He replied that he had used those years ago and was not satisfied. I asked if it was my Andersen that he had used. He said he was sure that it was. I could not believe it. Seldom had I ever seen a customer disgruntled with an Andersen product.

I asked if he could take me to the particular job and show me the window. I was surprised that he could and did. All I had to do was look at the trade mark on the sash lock and tell that it was not my product. It was the other Anderson. While I still lost the sale, I was happy that it was not my product that he was unhappy with.

Hal and Tensia Bastin selling Andersen windows in 2000 at Rupp Arena

Chapter 14

The Second Diversification: Kent and Kevin 1986-Current

By 1986 I realized that the great profits of the independent lumberyards were coming to a close. There was still profit in this business, but only the efficient would manage to survive. Could I be one of those? We had survived a recession that many thought was worse than the Great Depression of 1929. We have had stiff competition every year of our existence.

However, by the mid 1980's the chain yards were in all of the surrounding towns. Richmond, Danville and Somerset all had at least one chain yard. I knew that it would not be long before Nicholasville would have one also. Eighty-four Lumber would soon be entering the local market from several sides. It would not be easy, new challenges would surface and formidable obstructions would be in place.

While there were services that I could perform for the average builder, I could not get the normal mark up of twenty-six to twenty-eight percent. It would be more like twenty-one to twenty-two percent. Out of every one hundred dollars I would sell, I would have to get by on a mark up of twenty-two dollars. This would even be difficult sometimes.

Why not have ways out if necessary? I did not want to retire from the business that I loved especially since I had young boys that might want a business to go into once they were older. I had this opportunity given to me and I wanted to be able to pass it on to my sons Kent and

Kevin. But, exactly what business would I be giving them? Something to do with building, of course.

I had some contractors that had just built over one hundred homes and had given us all of their business. They asked me to buy two lots in Nicholasville from them to help them get a small duplex project on its way. At first I was negative toward this idea. My father had always said that he would never own apartments because they were too much trouble.

Any business that you get in, if lucrative, is difficult. If it was easy, someone else would have tried it long ago. I thought that I would give it a try and start off with two duplexes that would have two bedrooms. They were easy to build and Nicholasville had excellent potential. While it was a twenty mile trip one way, it would be a different type of business than I was used to. You couldn't go wrong with just two and if it proved difficult, I could always sell them and get a small profit.

The first two did fairly well with few problems, so the next year I bought two more lots on an adjacent street. My wife and I would go and clean them when someone moved and everything went well. Eight renters were no more of a problem than two. At least, it seemed that way. I kept signs up in the neighborhood and seemed to have a perpetual amount of phone calls. We had little down time and I almost forgot that I had them. My sons were in Little League baseball and I was coaching, so my lumber yard suffered more than the duplexes.

I will never regret the time I spent with my children in baseball. I coached for eight or nine years and the time had to come from somewhere. I appreciate my wife going along with the program, because of the difficulty of having a good business, good family life and the coaching. You do not have your children with you forever. More parents should be involved with their children and get to know them. While it might not be baseball or sports, it should be something wholesome they enjoy.

In the latter part of their baseball, our duplexes were doing excellent and there was no gripe about high prices and volatile lumber markets. In fact, rent would go up in a slow, steady rate. Our first rents on the first buildings were about $350 a month with a $200 deposit. Now the same duplex would rent for $490 a month with a $300 deposit. This was not a get rich quick business, but neither was the lumber business. It was something that would be a hedge against inflation. In America, this is what you must have as an investor. You can't just put your money on interest and sleep.

Another subdivision had opened up and we took four lots. The cost of building had gone up as did the lots. The duplex business was steady as it had always been. It took more time, but my wife liked to clean and paint them and I helped. While we liked Nicholasville, there were two lots in Danville that were available. Since she helped so willingly, I built her two duplexes in Danville. Too, they have performed well, but we both feel that we should have stayed in Nicholasville with all of our duplexes. For one thing, they would have all been together and centrally managed. More important, Nicholasville has more favorable laws about getting dead beats out that will not pay their rent.

In Nicholasville, you can have someone out that has not paid their rent in two weeks. In other towns, it might be two months, and the renters know this. We are careful to point this out to all new customers. We do not want to evict you, but will if the rent is not paid on time. In Nicholasville, we have not lost a case in eighteen years. Nicholasville is a town, friendly to business. Too, this makes it so we can rent at a lower price. It actually helps the renter.

I did not have the ready money to build such a large project lying around in the bank. NO! I had to borrow it from First Southern Bank through their able loan officer, McKinley Dailey. While McKinley and I are good friends, if I default on my payments, he will have to take my duplexes and sell them.

In 2000 more lots were available on the by-pass in Nicholasville. In fact, all of our duplexes were just off of the by-pass. I feel that this is why they have done so well. In fifteen to twenty minutes, you can be in Lexington. Now, we built five more duplexes. All were two bedroom duplexes. We do not build a garage because investigation taught us that tenants abused garages and leave them in bad shape when vacating. Instead, we built a two hundred eighty cubic foot storage building in the rear of our new duplexes. In fact, if you examine all of the one car garages in duplexes that furnish them ninety percent of the time they are used for storage. We took a survey to determine this factor.

While we do not discriminate against children, we find that they are more destructive than most animals. Perhaps I should not point out this controversial point, but in writing this book, I want to express the ideas and practices that developed our businesses. I hope no one would say that our family does not like children. We have plenty of them. Actually, I do not think I would want to rent to my children as adolescents. I know that I would not want to rent to my brother and me when we were small.

If you have three bedroom apartments, I feel that you are asking for trouble. This is just my feeling. Thank goodness there are three and four bedroom apartments for people who need them. Most every month, I fail to pick up a good renter because I do not have a three bedroom duplex. On the other hand, it is much easier to clean a two bedroom. For our family, we specialize in two bedroom duplexes.

The rental business did so well for us that in 2004, we made our largest expansion ever. For us, this was big. First, we had to talk the bank into going along with the project. I did not know how they would like our idea. Did they have confidence in me and my family with so large a project? I had never borrowed this much money! By this time, I had long positioned my lumber business to the point that I did not need to borrow large sums of money to keep it going. In the busy months I might have to, but, not like building thirty-two new duplexes in the form of sixteen buildings.

When people pay their rent, they have no idea of the debt that the landlord must incur. They seem to think he just goes off with the months rent and spends it. In eighteen years, my family has always placed one hundred percent of the money in the banks hands. Too, we have had expenses such as property taxes, insurance, and interest. Also, furnaces, air conditioners, and roofs go bad and must be repaired. Few customers will treat the property like their own. Many will allow their children to mark the walls and to pull off cabinet doors. After expenses, we place the balance against the principal. If you do it any other way, I feel that you are headed for trouble. This is why the duplex business is not just for anyone. I have had many people come up to me and ask my advice on getting into this line of work. Some people who work with us on repair feel that we are getting rich fast and for this reason, they have started duplexes on their own. Even people of some wealth and knowledge of investments have tried. Many have been disappointed and regretful of their decision to get into this field. Again, it is not for all people.

Like any other adventure in life, you must be prepared for disappointments and downturns. However, if you like to work with people and be of service to them, it can be rewarding. Since the very start of this business, I have included my children in the labor portion of the business. Kent and Kevin each have had jobs and responsibilities. They have learned to do them well enough to keep the business going well. In fact, they do all the jobs much better than I do now. Each one has a different job when one duplex becomes empty. One takes the stove and refrigerator and the other paints, while I might vacuum and make sure all materials for cleaning are on location. You must work on weekends and some at night. While the competition is different than lumber business, there are many duplexes for rent.

When someone wants to find a duplex, they have about five or six phone numbers they can call. They will normally go with the person that answers the phone first, with the most knowledge about his product and a tone of courtesy in their voice. We try to describe the amenities in our buildings and not oversell.

By the turn of the century in 2000, people did not want gas heat. Twenty years ago, this was the thing to have, as houses stayed warmer with gas heat, and it was inexpensive. You did not even need good insulation with gas heat. It is different now. No one wants gas heat. The few units that we have with gas heat rent at a discount. It would almost be profitable to change them to an electric furnace.

However, what goes up might come down. It is possible that gas heat will come down to where it was several years ago. We will not convert as long as we can rent the gas heated out at a reasonable price. When that time comes, we will find a contractor who will convert all of our old ones to electric. At this time, the cost would be about four thousand dollars a building. This cost is going up all the time since electric furnaces, by law, have to become more efficient.

In January 2004 we started our first duplex in Squire Lakes Subdivision, just off Highway 27 by-pass in Nicholasville. We picked out sixteen lots with the same floor plan in mind. We used the same pattern of carpet as well as the same decor for the interior. We used what would clean up and paint quick. We allow no wall paper or border. If you allow renters to put up border you are asking for trouble. We will not allow any paint except what we sell. They must get any paint they want to touch up with from us and, of course, it is the same flat antique white. However, we give them the paint. They do not have to buy it. Most do well with it. If they want their deposit back, they must present the duplex back in the same shape as when they moved in. The only thing we tell them is that we expect normal ware and tare and expect to have to paint.

We try to delineate everything we expect of the renter that might move into the building. Sometimes I have lost good, young renters because I have told them that I will not put up with overly loud music and parties. I explain that there is no sense in moving in and then being scolded for something that will disturb a family that lives next door and wants some sleep. Sometimes in my zeal to avoid future problems, I have lost good, young renters. Be that as it may, we still had rather explain the essentials of community living at the outset rather than have problems later.

Experience has taught us that it is wise to look over each potential renter and follow up on their references before making a hasty decision. My sons are good at computers and look at the court docket in Nicholasville each week. If someone is being taken to small claims court it is likely that they are not paying their rent. If they are being evicted from one place, it is likely that they will bring you trouble also.

We have had people come to us and say that our price for rent is too high. They declare that they can rent a town house for thirty five dollars a month less than our price. Sure, I say. But look at the problems with a town house. They are two story and you have people living on all sides of you. In our duplex, you have your own front, back and side yards. Too, you have only one renter to put up with. If you rent a townhouse, you probably rent from a large company that might have its office in Lexington or Louisville. With us, you can reach me on my cell phone at any time. We are quick to answer any problems and have contractors to handle any problems. I have talked with people who tell me that they can not even get their property manager to return their call. The roof might be leaking and no one will take the call to make the repairs. This is something that the property owner would want to know before damage would be done to the interior of the duplex.

Many times when my phone rings, I feel frustrated when they ask me if I am busy. Of course I am busy! But, I never act like I am upset. You must know how to fake it and act pleasant. Most of the time we manage to do this.

I do not always judge a renter by the way they dress. I have gained some excellent renters that were sloppy and perhaps needed a bath. You must take all things into consideration.

While duplexes are the main business we have diversified with, there is one other business we have taken a small position in. This is speculative home building. In 2005 and 2006 we have built about nine houses of about fifteen hundred square feet. They have sold well, but we will not stay in this business since it represents some very mild competition with our regular building customers. Some of them feel that we can build much cheaper than they can since we buy the materials cheaper. This is not actually true since they perform many of the facets of home building more efficiently than we can.

Unless something else comes along, we will stay with renting and being material buyers. I can actually say that our family loves both businesses.

L to R-Kevin Bastin, Kent Bastin and Rickey Gonzalez at a duplex in Nicholasville 2001

Chapter 15

Funny and Amusing Happenings

There are many funny and amusing stories that I could glean over from over the forty years I have been at Bastin Lumber. One of the best stories centers on my foreman telling me that we were missing lumber over the weekends. We were sure who the culprit was and I had the perpetrator charged with the theft of the missing lumber. He was lacking in education and quite poor and I almost dropped the charges. His court appointed lawyer did an excellent job in defending him and I was surprised that the judge asked for more evidence. We could never put our finger on any particular item that he had stolen. We only could prove he was in the lumber yard after closing time, and that was on several occasions. We could not find the stash of stolen goods to really make our case. Finally, when the judge declared the man acquitted, he asked if that meant he would have to give the lumber back.

One time when I was trying to convince my Father of my ability as a salesman, we discussed methods of selling. I confessed that there was a certain customer that I simply could not sell. I could not pry him away from my competitor. My Dad said not to give up and try something different. Several weeks later my Father asked if I had a plan for this particular situation. I said, "Yes!" I will promise him lower prices, better delivery and top quality. I will tell him that as sure as the sun sets in the West, he will be happy with us as a supplier. Dad said, "Son, if the sun doesn't set in the West, there won't be any need to even talk to him."

Not long after I took over the management of the lumber yard I had to go to Louisville and examine two box car load of framing lumber. While it was not ours yet, it was still not sold. A possible bargain! I was told it was dirty from weather exposure but, other than that, it was fine. Just make a counter offer. I had to fly to Atlanta later in the day so a trip to Louisville and time would not be wasted. I took old clothes with me to examine the lumber at the railroad yards and would have just enough time to go to my hotel to change and catch the flight to Atlanta.

I examined the lumber and declined to purchase it since there was more damage than expressed in the original conversation. I went back to my hotel and as I walked through the lobby I noticed that it had changed from my check in time. Something was different. There was a strange smell of flowers. Since I was in a hurry, I went straight to the elevator and to the fourth or fifth floor to clean up. I could not have been more than twenty to twenty-five minutes and hit the elevator with a raincoat in one arm and my suitcase in the other.

When I walked out of the elevator a surprise awaited me. In the few minutes that I spent cleaning up, a marriage had been set up in the lobby! To my right stood the minister and bride and groom, to my left stood at least fifty wedding guests. I had no idea at first exactly what was going on. I heard organ music. I immediately took off my hat and place it over my heart. This brought giggles from the gathering. Then I tried to back into the elevator. Too late! The door closed. My face turned various colors of red. The minister stayed cool and moved the proceedings on to its conclusion. I just stood there between the sacred proceedings and all of these people that I had never seen before.

Finally, after what seemed three years, they were pronounced man and wife, and I eased my way through the smiling crowd and was told that my appearance came exactly when the minister asked if there were any reasons for this couple not being joined in marriage.

The whole group of people were very nice and seemed to take the humor well. In fact, after being introduced to the bride and groom and minister, they expressed delight in the unusual interruption. They apologized to me since it was unusual for someone to be married in a hotel lobby.

Perhaps the strangest occurrence came in 1975. At this time Barbara Ray was my secretary. She lived at the end of Mt. Hebron Road in the northern end of the county. It seemed that this was at least eighteen miles away. It's a journey over several different narrow roads that I had never been completely over.

At this time, I was breeding bloodhounds. I had a nice female that I had picked up in South Carolina. I placed an ad in the Lexington paper and sure enough, a nice girl from Lawrenceburg answered the ad with a promise to bring over her stud to see if we could get some pups. The deal was that she got the first pup as her fee. That was all. She examined my pen and female dog, Sunshine. After she was confident that I was a responsible host, she stated that this one hundred forty pound dog of hers was worth five thousand dollars! Was I sure that I could manage the pair of them? After leaving her phone number, she went back to Lawrenceburg with a promise that I would call her when something happened.

I thought my female was in heat. Nothing seemed to happen. A week passed and still the dogs showed no interest in each other. Every day when I returned to my farm on Old Danville Road, I would check them out. Still nothing happened. I called her to tell her that perhaps she should come over and get her valuable dog since nothing was working out. She said that she would be over Tuesday night. This was only forty-eight hours away. Monday morning when I got up, as I went to examine the dogs, I noticed the gate open! Her dog was gone and mine was in the yard. After putting my female back in her pen, I started to panic. Where was this five thousand dollar dog? Why did I accept the responsibility for such a high priced animal? In fact, I wasn't really a breeder of dogs at all. Where could this mutt be?

I looked all over my sixty acre farm but, no bloodhound. I called up neighbors, but no one had seen such a large dog. When I arrived at the lumber yard, I confessed my plight to Barbara Ray and all who would listen. Where could this dog be? I called the police station and the sheriff's office. No clue. I remember going to eat lunch with Ronnie Cormney at the Country Diner. After I lamented my situation to him, he smiled and said that he saw a large dog, like you see on the TV show, HEE HAW, walking out on Lexington Street early that morning.

Ronnie and I joked a lot with each other, so I did not take him serious at first. Every time I would ask him if he was serious, he could not seem to help laughing. I did not know if he was laughing at my situation with the girl or what. I told him that I was in big trouble if I did not have that dog back by Tuesday evening when she would come to pick him up.

While the rest of the day was busy at the lumber yard, it was overbearing on my mind. What would I tell her? Why did I get into this mess?

Keep in mind that my secretary, Barbara Ray had never seen the dog. She had never come close to him. No contact at all. Not only that, but she lived in the complete opposite direction of where the dog's home was in Lawrenceburg. No rime or reason for it to go north of town, especially north East.

About six thirty pm that evening, Barbara called me and said that a large dog was at her house and that it just might be the dog that I was looking for. While a ray of hope came across my aspirations, common sense reflected that this was near impossible. After Barbara described the dog, I knew I had to see for myself. How could this happen? A bloodhound that would defy all odds and go to a home that knew what type of situation I was in. One in a million! It was a trip of about eighteen miles in one direction. This trip was made from about nine am in the morning, when Ronnie saw the dog, and six pm when it arrived at the unlikely home of someone who knew my situation.

I took my pick up truck and navigated US 27 North to Mt. Hebron Road and the remaining several miles to Barbara's home. Sure enough! It was the male bloodhound that I was looking for. While a one hundred forty pound bloodhound looks imposing, most of them are quite gentle. Only don't bother them while they eat. I pushed him into the shotgun side of the truck and after thanking Barbara and her husband, raced back to my farm.

I immediately placed the two dogs together. I tied the gates in four places and left the rest to nature. They acted like long lost lovers immediately! Now, I had to keep the status quo for another twenty-four hours. Maybe I would not have to confess my embarrassment to this nice lady who loved her dog so much. Every hour or so, I would go and check to see if the dogs were still there, if they needed water.

The next morning I called the lady and told her to make sure to arrive early, that we had success. Perhaps we could expect pups in about two months. Sure enough, she arrived about five pm and seemed happy about my report of the dogs breeding. While nothing could be guaranteed, I told her that I would call her as soon as any results were evident. I did not tell her about the strange occurrence. The epilogue to the story was good and bad. Good in that Sunshine had twelve pups. Bad in that I was unable to register the one she picked out. Why, I still do not know. Somehow, I just messed up the papers every time I sent them in. The lady got mad and frustrated with me. No telling what she would have done if I had not found her dog.

Another amusing happening that involved me in Lancaster came when a lawyer friend of mine, John E. Smith, and I drove to Birmingham, Alabama in 1970 to see Bear Bryant's Alabama team lose to Southern California in a high scoring thriller. On the way to Birmingham, John drove his Corvette at speeds of ninety to one hundred miles per hour! I was white knuckles to the dash board and applying imaginary brakes. I even asked to drive. I begged him to slow down, but, to no avail. The only thing that worked was to talk him into a wager of some kind. We could not get a bet up on the game, so we started talking baseball. He was a Braves fan from way back. We spoke of Alvin Dark, a Rookie of the year for the Braves in 1948 when he batted .322 and hit thirty-nine doubles. Dark was a favorite of mine especially when he was traded to the Giants and helped in the amazing come back of 1951 to win the pennant. I thought that I knew more about Dark's career than most anyone.

First one statement led to another and I stated that Dark only played for two teams, the Braves and the Giants. John said definitely not! He played for the Cubs and Cardinals as well as for the Phillies. I could not picture this. So I noticed that while we were arguing, he slowed down to about eighty or eighty-five. Anyway I could, I extended the argument. However, John finally got tired of bickering and said put up or shut up! I will bet fifty dollars that Dark played for at least three teams besides the Braves. Now, the Corvette was back up to about one hundred miles per hour on a two lane road in rural Alabama. All right, I said. Slow down and we will frame a wager up. As he slowed down again we decided on a fifty dollar bet. While I was against betting, it might have saved my life in this instance.

I stalled and re-phrased the bet as long as I could before a final agreement was made. Now, I was not sure of myself, but we arrived in Birmingham in one piece. Since the game the next day was at night, we went to a bookstore to spend some idle time. All of a sudden, I came across a baseball encyclopedia that had all statistics of every player since 1900. I pushed the book back where John might not see it to prove his case or mine. I was afraid now, especially since John seemed more confident every time the subject was brought up. Well, the worst happened. John fumbled through the sports books and found the book of statistics. In seconds, he had proved me wrong and demanded his fifty dollars. While I learned a good lesson in this experience, I would do the same thing over again to slow that Corvette down.

The story does not end there. Several years later, I found that an old friend of mine, Ford Philpot was going to hold a protracted meeting at the Methodist Church in Lancaster. I had a religious radio program in Cynthiana of my own where Ford preached in 1957. I had attended many of his crusades throughout the years and found him to be the one of the best evangelists in this part of the country.

This was about 1981, at least eleven years after the trip that John and I took to Alabama. Before arriving at the Methodist Church, I was pleased to find out that Ford had arranged to have Alvin Dark flown in from California to give a testimony. I could not believe it! Can you imagine the wheels that were turning in my mind? On the way to the church I found that John would be working in his office close to where the Court House Annex is located now. I told him to sit tight until nine pm, that I had important business with him. Never mind what, it was, but just wait until nine or nine-thirty pm.

After the nice service by Reverend Philpot, I made sure that I was the last to greet Alvin Dark. Fortunately, most everyone left when I exchanged introductions with the great L.S.U. halfback and athlete. I asked him to step up the street for just a minute and I would have him back in no time at all. Things worked out perfect. Can you imagine John's face when he saw this baseball hero and subject of our earlier wager come into his office! In fact, if I had had time, I am sure I could have won the fifty dollars back with some sort of a bet on having Alvin Dark in John's office.

Baseball is the past time of America, and always will be. My father, Hob, was a rabid Cincinnati Reds fan, as I am and my sons also. Kevin and Kent live for the day when we see the Reds play in Cincinnati. We watch all games together on TV and live and die with the Reds. I played American Legion baseball as well as high school baseball and loved the game. I have coached baseball in Georgia in the 1960's and in Little League in Lancaster with my sons.

One of the biggest thrills came at Bastin Lumber Company, however. In 1966, not long after I took over the management of the lumber company, the L & N Railroad agent came into the lumber yard and asked how long I would be staying past five pm. He declared that he had an important package for a gentleman from Madison County and had promised to wait until he arrived to pick it up. Since the agent was now on overtime, he asked if I would keep the package until he came to pick it up. If so, he would write a note on the depot, just next to my business, to instruct him to come to the lumber yard to pick it up. After agreeing to this, I did not ask who the customer might be.

I remember it was in winter time and it might have been snowing. In a few minutes a tall, gray headed man came in and asked if there was a package for Earl Combs there. I asked Earl Combs? Was he the Earl Combs that played for the Yankees with Babe Ruth and Lou Gehrig? Yes, he declared. "I am what is left of him". Actually, Earl Combs was in the class with Ruth and Gehrig. In fact, he is one of the first of center fielders with the Yankees that featured Combs, Joe DiMaggio and Mickey Mantle. He played with the Yankees from 1924 until 1935 and was inducted into the Hall of Fame in Cooperstown in 1970 and had a lifetime batting average of .325. I was especially impressed with the time he took to talk to me about baseball. I wish at this time I possessed a camera. In only ten years, this Kentucky hero would pass on to the next life.

Between the years of 1968 and 1974 a gentleman from the Siple Brick Company in Stanton, Kentucky called on me about once a month. During this period we bought brick wholesale. Brick companies do not like to do this now. They sell direct to the customer or go through a jobber. I was not real sad when we stopped selling brick, since we only got a ten percent mark up on it and then had to carry it on our books for another month or two.

Vic Bradford was the salesman that called on me during these years of mass selling of masonry products. While I was a good customer of the Siple Brick Company and glad to see Vic, we spent little time talking about building materials.

Vic was the starting quarterback on the undefeated Alabama football team of 1934. Alabama ran an old Notre Dame Box type of offense where the quarterback mostly blocked. Still, he was a great player and I enjoyed his visits more for football talk than a chance to buy good brick at a low price.

Vic almost went into coaching as a full time vocation instead of selling brick for his wife's family business. While he was an excellent salesman, I felt that he had missed his real calling as a coach.

In 1950 Vic was a defense coach of the best team that Kentucky has ever put on a field. Paul Bear Bryant had been the head coach for four years and pushed UK to the apex of their football experience. They were the national champions of the 1950 season by defeating Oklahoma thirteen to seven in the Sugar Bowl in New Orleans. I remember listening to the game as a child. Never again, has Kentucky gained this status.

While Bear Bryant was the best head coach ever, he had assembled the most promising coaching staff at the University in 1950 and 1951 that one could imagine. There was Ermal Allen from Cynthiana. I personally knew him and followed his career through his stint with the Dallas Cowboys. While not a head coach, pound for pound, this scrappy assistant coach was an able helper. Next, Paul Dietzel, who later led LSU to a national championship, coached the offense. Too, Charlie McClendon, who played at UK, was on the staff. He took over at LSU when Dietzel left and went to West Point. Next, there was Jim Owens who coached the Washington Huskies to Pac Ten fame. Bryant's long time assistants, Carney Laslie and Buckshot Underwood rounded out this staff that Vic Bradford was part of.

Anytime I knew that Vic would stop by, I always made at least an hour of free time. One of the games we talked about most was the last major bowl that UK played in: the January 1, 1952 Cotton Bowl, when the Cats defeated Texas Christian twenty to seven. Few of us realized that this would be their last big bowl game, perhaps forever. Let's hope that his drought ends soon.

We always got on the 1951 Sugar Bowl game where Kentucky defeated Oklahoma thirteen to seven and vaulted into national fame. Vic helped Bear devise a defense against

Oklahoma that used four tackles. This was a gamble since Oklahoma had won thirty-one straight games and might be considered a dynasty. Coach Bud Wilkinson had perfected the split-T behind an array of All American talent. This Bradford inspired defense brought up his corner backs and created a virtual nine-man line. With this, UK had defeated the national champions and ended the longest winning streak in college football. It was good for the lumber yard when Vic Bradford quit calling on us in about 1975. As you can imagine, a whole afternoon might be wasted.

Bastin Lumber Company was always interested in sports. I remembered finding an old baseball jersey that had Bastin Lumber written on the front of it and Buckeye written on the back. My uncle, Ross Bastin had sponsored this team from Buckeye, but I could not find out any statistics on the team or what age group was sponsored.

Hob, Bob Goff and Ross did not do much in the area of sponsorship. In 1990 my oldest son, Kevin, was eligible to play in a pre Little League program at the Jaycees Baseball Park. I was asked to sponsor and did. I made sure I did not second guess the coach since I would resent anyone doing this to me. Kevin had a good time with this program and wanted to play in the Little League program the next year.

Tom Hurt was managing this program and asked me to sponsor

and coach, if I would promise to stay at least two years. I ended up staying seven more years.

The first year I inherited a few good players, but they did not like to practice. Several quit. One excellent player, a shortstop, was All Star material, but likes to gripe at umpires and accuse them of cheating. I would not put up with this. In this stage of baseball, a manager should never throw a fit or yell at an umpire. I am amazed at the ones who do. I will not put up with it. This child quit as soon as he saw that I would take the umpire's side.

We were not left with much. We finished third in a four team league. Kevin made the All Star team and was selected to pitch by Eric May and Curt Carrier. I was very proud of him. As usual, our All Star team did not do well. Eric and Curt did an outstanding job, but we do not have the number of kids to choose from that larger teams have. Usually it is in the area of pitching that we have trouble.

The next year I was lucky to be able to pick Nick Sullivan. While this is only a two year program, I was loaded with talent for our last year of Kevin's eligibility. We won the league and I was All Star coach. Trouble again. We had some excellent hitters, but little in pitching. Too, one of our best players went on vacation. Since he was the best pitcher in the league, we were lucky to split our all star games. Please note that our league was not sanctioned. We just played independent teams.

McKinley Dailey helped me coach this all star team. We got along well and he would work hard. I feel that McKinley was one of the best coaches for the kids at the park.

In 1993, Kevin Bastin went to the Pony League for boys in the age group between thirteen and fifteen. This was the first time in several years that the park had teams for this age group. We all enjoyed it and played some good baseball. I coached one year in this league, since my youngest son, Kent was still in a minor league.

In 1994, I came back to coach Kent and some of his friends in his first year of Little League. I was intense and practiced all of my teams hard. We would practice at least twice a week and play twice. I hope I taught them some good fundamentals of the game. I would go by my experiences in baseball as a catcher in American Legion, as well as a center fielder. Too, I went to the bookstore to get the latest books on instructions on how to coach each position. It had been twenty five years since I had coached in Atlanta. Baseball is not a static game. It is ever changing and flexible. Any coach that does not do this is doing a disservice to his team. The same is true in business, just because you might know how to win today, next year; another coach will try a new technique and beat you.

In 1994, our team did really well. The trouble was that we had to play Eric and Curt again and they were loaded. Out of five games with this bunch, we won the third and fourth games while losing all of the rest. We won all of the rest of our games to finish twelve and three. I kept and still have all of our stats on all of these games. Eric and Curt won the tournament as well. They should have coached the All Stars, but asked me to do the job. After Shelby Hopkins agreed to help me, I consented. We had good talent and again, split our decisions in this post season play. Shelby went at the game just about like I did. He was very intense and ready to win. One of the things that hurt in this experience was that I would seldom see any of these people after coaching. You make good friends and as soon as the baseball is over you do not see much of them again.

I remember Bill and Debbie Craddock. They put in more time with a wonderful attitude than any civic couple I ever met. They took the hard jobs that no one else wanted. I would not manage one of these leagues for any amount of money. It was bad enough coaching. They made fair decisions that were sometimes unpopular with about half of the people. Their decisions were always fair. I do not know how many hours they worked in the several years that they put in. The town should appreciate the work people like this do. They did it all.

The year 1995, was Kent Bastin's last year in Little League. We had Chris Davis, Kevin Crutchfield, Zach Adams, Josh Underwood, and Jeremy Brogli to go with others to make a perfect seventeen and zero record. We won all of our games as well as two tournament games. This would be our first year as a sanctioned team in All Stars. The problem was that there was not a lot of talent in the league. I had seven of the starters on my team. Believe me; I would play anyone in order to win a game. The talent was just not there. Out of about eight All Star games, we only won one. I did not have Shelby to help me this year and was worn out after a game or practice.

I coached and sponsored teams with Kent and my step-son, Ricky Gonzalez in the Pony League in 1996 and 1997. During this eight year tenure I probably lost a lot of money by not being at my business. No doubt about it. However, I would not take anything for the experience I had with my three boys. The best thing was that they never fell out with me. They were very pleasant to be around while we played and coached together. My wife didn't know anything about baseball, coming from Costa Rica. I am grateful that she put up with the lot of us.

The only regrets that I had during this period centered on kids that did not get to play as much as they would have liked. I had to take several lectures from parents that were disgusted with my style of selection of who played and for how long. I do not blame them. When you have charge of the most precious thing a parent has, you are on dangerous ground. Always, I would jut listen and say little. The angry parent is probably right in the first place. The trouble is that they all can not play at once. I hope the people that I offended during this time will forgive me.

In this phase of coaching, I was not the best coach. In any case, after Kent and Ricky were out of the age to coach, my wife and I were happy campers. I would not take anything for the memories, but would never do it again. I was sixty when I quit. This is usually a grandparent's age. My

Dad was forty-three when I was born and I was forty-three when Kevin was born. I do not recommend this age gap to coaches.

From 1973 to 1979 Evans Products, a national building materials and plywood chain of wholesale products sent a salesman to call on me by the name of Wilbur Shu. He lived in Georgetown and would call on me about twice a month. Wilbur played and started on the 1944-45 and the 1945-46 teams of UK that ended up being the SEC champions. He played forward and center in a few circumstances. Wilbur was about 6'6" which was big for those days.

Adolph Rupp, the UK coach, wrote a letter to his assistant, while he was serving a stint in the Navy, pointing out that Wilbur Shu was the best forward that UK had. Too, for some reason Wilbur was ineligible for a portion of the season. Rupp was worried about this since he was an excellent player.

Like the other sports celebrities that might stop by, Wilbur would always tell me a good sports story. In his case, it would be about Adolph Rupp, the legendary coach of the Cats. Rupp was much like Bear Bryant of football fame in that he was full of himself. He was such a venerable coach it was possible to be and act this way.

While Wilbur told many funny and amusing stories about Coach Rupp, the best one occurred after he graduated. It was when Kentucky visited St. Louis to play the Billikens and their feisty coach, Ed Hickey. While Hickey was a great coach, Rupp hated him. For good reason! Hickey's teams had defeated UK three times in the Sugar Bowl basketball tournament. In those days they would have a basketball game that would go along with the football Sugar Bowl. Generally, UK would go and several times play the St. Louis Billikens. Wilbur was on one of those teams that lost to St. Louis and remembered that Rupp was unforgiving in his appraisal of any UK team that lost to the hated Coach Hickey.

Too, the last three games against St. Louis were lost by only a grand total of four points. Shu said that Coach Rupp referred to Coach Hickey as a little slob. The hatred was that bad. While UK won this particular game by a 71-59 score, a funny thing happened that could not happen today.

Coach Hickey's son was the official timer. In those days, games were played in quarters. Young Hickey fired a blank cartridge to signal a timeout, end of quarter, or end of the game. The seating arrangement placed both teams on the sideline where the end of the line of the Kentucky squad was the start of the St. Louis squad. Hickey's son, sat right next to UK's assistant coach, Harry Lancaster. At the time, Coach Lancaster had no idea just who he was sitting next too.

When the first quarter ended, young Hickey placed the revolver right next to Lancaster's leg and fired. A wad of whatever came out and the coach said it hurt like hell. When Coach Lancaster told him not to do that again, young Hickey cursed him. Sure enough, when the half ended, Hickey shot the UK assistant again in the same place. Harry, being referred to as Rupp's bouncer, smacked the slightly built Hickey and knocked him several feet across the basketball floor.

With this, fans from St. Louis, coaches and others came running out on the floor and caused pandemonium. Several UK fans that tried to come to the aid of Coach Lancaster were sent to the St. Louis jail. Rupp, Lancaster and the UK staff had to be helped to the dressing room by police escort. They wanted to take Harry to jail because young Hickey was still dazed. However, the Kentucky Athletic Director, Burnie Shively, persuaded the police to let him stay for the rest of the game.

For once in his life, Coach Rupp ate humble pie and talked Coach Hickey into allowing Harry Lancaster to avoid a trip to jail. When Wilbur would tell this story, tears would come to his eyes when he came to the part about young Hickey shooting Lancaster with cork or something. It was funny.

While I was in high school in Cynthiana, I would play on the local American Legion baseball team. I remember that I was fifteen year old and, of course, could not have a driver's license. We needed transportation since we would play in Lexington at least four times a year.

The Sheriff of the county was the father of Joe B. Hall, later to become the UK basketball coach. Joe B. was from Cynthiana. His family had a flower business and delivered in a truck fashioned much like a UPS delivery truck. Perhaps it was not as large, but on the same line. It was a straight transmission, since few trucks in those days had automatic.

At fifteen years of age, I would go to the good Sheriff and ask to borrow his truck. The reply was that he would do anything for the youth of the county and tell us that we would not be allowed to even put gas in it. He would furnish everything, everything but the driver. I learned to drive a straight shift on this Sheriff's truck at fifteen years old. Well, not completely. While I drove and pushed on the clutch, another player changed the gears.

My Father never found out about this. Neither did Bill Hall, the Sheriff. No telling what he might have done if he knew that I didn't have a license. Years later, when I told Joe B, he just laughed.

The final basketball story that I remember involved another good player among the greatest. Dutch Campbell was a forward on Rupp's 1946 team that ranked among his best. While Dutch was not a regular, he was good and could start at most any college in the nation. I did not know Dutch until the spring of 1955 when he practiced his Harrison County High baseball team in the same location as our Cynthiana team practiced. We had to share Lawson field. We were town rivals and, as you could imagine, threats and challenges would be expressed the whole time the field was shared.

I remember the Harrison County Coach, Dutch Campbell walking over to our portion of the field and declaring that he, at about thirty one years of age, could outrun anybody on our team. He would bet any amount of money on it.

When he loudly proclaimed this all over the athletic field, I tried to size him up. While he was big and still looked like he had been an athlete, I thought that I could beat him in a hundred yard dash. I did not have ten dollars to lose. I would worry about that later. I hollered at this modern day Goliath and told him I'd take him up. I remember asking my baseball coach, Jimmy Cinnamon, "How fast is he?" I do not remember Coach Cinnamon's reply.

I remember the cold spring day we lined up on the adjacent football field and getting ready to race for ten dollars. I realized that I had better win since I had no money with me. I was in good shape, since I ran sprints regularly. I had learned to run while at Kentucky Military School. They made us run six miles a day if we played football. I kept this up when I returned home to Cynthiana.

It was an easy race. Coach Campbell probably was not in as good of shape as he thought. I won by perhaps ten yards. Too, I collected the ten dollars. This was a large amount of money for 1955.

Chapter 16

Geography

Notes on the lots that compose Bastin Lumber Inc and the dates they were obtained.

The house lot is now on, 201 South Campbell Street. This is the home of Hal and Tensia Bastin. The house was built in 1872 by Hiram Wortham. It was purchased for the Bastin family in 1900 by Hal's grandfather, Alford. This lot measures about 74' x 75'. This was the original office of Bastin Lumber Company in 1914. It remained so until 1946 when the office was located at its present location of 203 South Campbell Street.

The upstairs of 201 S. Campbell Street was used as a residence and the downstairs was used as a store/office. Alford Bastin, Hob Bastin, Bob and Mayme Goff used this in the residence over the years. When Bob Goff died in 1943, Hob Bastin moved the Geoghegan family upstairs for a residence while Tom Geoghegan worked at the lumber yard. His wife Eva took care of Mayme Goff.

In 1952, the house was remodeled, and twelve feet got cut off the front of the store building for a front yard, and both floors were used as a residence. My Aunt Mayme moved in downstairs and Ross's sister-in-law, Sue Anna Rose moved in upstairs. Sue Anna was the wife of Dr. Bascom C. Rose who was killed in a car accident at the Bryantsville Methodist Church in 1927.

Mayme Bastin Goff lived in this house until her death in 1978. At this time, I rented it out to various parties, including a law office of Henry Clay Cox and John E. Smith.

In 2000, my wife and I sold our farm on Old Danville Road and moved into this thirty-six hundred square foot home. This house has been owned by only two families since just after the Civil War, the Worthams and Bastins.

Bastin Lumber Company moves south. Well, not to Georgia or Alabama, but just to the next two lots. Lots #1, #2, and #3 that compose most of the land that our business is located on at the present time was bought at a master commissioner's sale in November of 1937. At that time, Bob Goff and Hob Bastin bought the three lots that are indicated on the map as Lots 1, 2, and 3. These lots were idle until just after the Second World War when the main office was moved from across the street to its present day location. It measures 70' x 30'. This property had been owned by the Seymour Hopper Estate and had been in their family since the Civil War.

As soon as World War II was over, when building materials and blacktop became available, my father built sheds #1 and #2 between the store rooms that had been moved. Too, he built a 40' x 30' concrete block building that would store various materials. Walden & Grubbs performed their first blacktop job on all of the grounds that were not covered with buildings.

The Louisville and Nashville Railroad laid a private spur track along the side of our

100 x 20 shed. My Uncle Ross Bastin was in good position to operate a small, country lumber yard.

In 1966 I added a 30' x 30' office and additional sales room to the old store room. Too, I rebuilt the 70' x 90' lower shed and prepared it for fork lift operation. We now had a lumberyard that was suitable for the operation of a fork lift.

The property remained the same until Bill Taulbee's warehouse burned in 1982. It had been a warehouse for many years that stored hemp, grain, fertilizer and related farm merchandise. Bill bought it in about 1971. I bought it from Bill's estate in 1982. The City of Lancaster gave me a quick claim deed to the alley if I would relieve them of the job of street repair.

I immediately built a 30' x 60' metal storage building where I planned to warehouse OSB boards and plywood. It worked well since it already had a nice concrete floor. J. K. Simpson and I divided up the railroad yards to where I added 30 more feet to the south of my property line. We have about two acres on the east side of Campbell Street, which is more than sufficient for my needs at this business.

Chapter 17

Bastin Lumber Co. and Banking: A Merchants Dream

My grandfather, Alford, immediately identified with the Citizens National Bank when he bought the phone company in this county in 1900. He was not a rich man by any means but could produce a financial statement of at least fifteen thousand dollars. This had come from the sale of a county store in Crab Orchard and a small farm that he and his wife inherited. Too, he saved some money form his school teaching in Lincoln County.

When his mother in law, Melinda Ross died in 1899 he was free to move to Lancaster and set up the phone company. While he did not need to borrow money to buy the phone company, he had to borrow to keep it up and running. Banks Hudson was the cashier of the Citizens at this time and was a good friend of Alford's. Everyone in town wanted my family to do well in this venture since it was a needed public service.

In 1912 Alford bartered the phone company for lumber. He needed a loan to buy other supplies for his new business. He stocked paint, tin roofing, shingles, hardware, sash and doors as well as lumber. He had to establish an accounts receivable and inventory. This took money until several turn over's took place and he was established.

He liberally used Banks Hudson, W.F. Champ, and Lewis Walker many times until he sold this business to my father and Bob Goff in 1921. At the time of the sale to Goff and Hob Bastin, Guy Davidson was the cashier and handled all of the Bastins business.   Remember, Guy Davidson was the first to see Clell Pointer (the man who shot Jim Hamilton in the duel) when he walked backed into town after the shooting in 1923.

My father and Bob Goff stayed with the Citizens Bank through the first years of their business partnership. When they bought the Harrison Lumber Co. in Cynthiana they borrowed money from George Hoskins, the man who sold them that business, and from Long Bell Lumber Co. out of Quitman, Mississippi. Since they bought that Harrison County concern at a bargain price, it did not take long to have it paid for.

When the 1929 Depression came, the partners were in good financial shape and not leveraged to any bank or lending institution. They did all of their Garrard County business at the Citizens Bank and their Harrison County business at the Farmers National Banks in Cynthiana.

Bastin and Goff made more money flipping property in the 1930's then working their lumber yards. They needed short term loans to manage this speculation and were able to get them at the Citizens Bank.

William Franklin Champ was the actual manager of this bank from about 1911 to his death in 1951. What he said was the law. If he said you got the money…you got it. The two lumbermen used this bank until Bob Goff died in 1943. At this time, my father moved the business over to the National Bank. He had a feeling that the Citizens Bank would expire when Mr. Champ passed on. It turned out that he was right. In any case, as soon as Mr. Champ died, the Citizens Bank merged with the National Bank.

In 1945, slightly more then a year after Bob Goff died, Hob switched all of the Basin Lumber business over to the National Bank. Hob liked John Askins, the chairman of the board and Charlie Thompson, the president. Charlie and Hob grew up and attended the Lancaster Grade School together and shared a mutual respect. Both Hob and Ross mourned Charlie's passing in 1954.

I possess a letter from Hob to the National Bank on March 8, 1945 guaranteeing any note signed by his brother, Ross Bastin. I think that this is the first time the business used the bank that we have stayed with for the next sixty two years.

By 1947, Paul Elliott, a cousin of ours, was moving fast through the ranks of authority of this lending institution to Vice President. Paul was the son of a doctor William Elliott who administered the final rites to Jim Hamilton. In fact, Paul married Jim Hamilton's niece, Eugenia Dunlap. In 1947 Willie Hugh Sanders was the cashier of the National Bank and began his move forward to ownership of a majority of its stock.

In 1952 the National Bank merged with the Citizens Bank. At least two of the most able employees of the Citizens Bank came over to work at the National Bank at this time. Bob Guyn and Joe Walker joined Webb Kelly and the above mentioned bankers to form an excellent staff at this outstanding bank.

Perhaps, I have failed to mention the most outstanding banker in Garrard County's history in tracing the history of our bank relations. William F. (Billy) Miller worked for the Citizens National Bank for several years in the 1920's and later took a position with the Citizens Union National Bank in Louisville. He was a good friend in the area of banking to my father since Hob was the Chairman of the Board of the Farmers National Bank in Cynthiana for a number of years. Billy Miller was only three years younger then my dad and saw to it that his bank in Cynthiana was taken care of when it needed money. I recall my father talking about Billy Miller and the positive influence that he generated in the area of Kentucky banks. Billy died in 1970. He always kept up a home just outside of Lancaster on highway 52, just east of Conns Lane.

In April of 1953, Paul Elliott was named president of the National Bank in the vacancy caused by the death of Charlie Thompson. Paul had several brothers that were prominent citizens of Lancaster and one, a lawyer, in Louisville. One of the brothers, Dunlap, was a friend of mine even though he quit the bank and managed the Chrysler-Dodge agency in Lancaster. We were loyal to this cousin and purchased cars and trucks from him.

When I arrived in Lancaster in 1965, Paul was the president of the bank and personally handled credit issues. While Mr. Elliott respected me in my new position of manager of the lumberyard, he made sure that my father signed all notes that our company made.

February 1967

I was not fortunate to have Paul around for long. Not long after this able banker reached the peak of his career a diabetic condition forced the amputation of his leg, leaving him in a wheel chair. I herd rumors that the other leg might have to be amputated as well. Tragedy of a worse nature prevented this. Only a month after his lovely wife, Eugenia, died of cancer, a fire broke out in his house, located just across Lexington Street from the Lancaster Elementary School. Paul and his mother in law, Hallie Dunlap perished in this fire. The Lancaster Building and Loan occupies this space now. It was a tragic loss to our family, the National Bank and the town.

Fortunately, Willie Hugh Sanders had controlling interest in the bank and the transition form Paul Elliott to Willie Hugh Sanders went smooth. Bob Guyn and Homer Profitt rounded out the team of bankers that my business dealt with during the 1970's. Again, an early passing of Homer Profitt in 1979 robbed the community and bank of an excellent employee. Not only were these banking officials helpful in the financial aspect of my business but they were good customers as well. They built houses and kept their business at home in Lancaster. I recall my father, who was a banker himself in Cynthiana, stating that the National Bank had three top men who could run any bank in the state. They were Willie

Hugh Sanders, Bob Guyn and Homer Profitt.

In 1986 Willie Hugh Sanders sold his bank stock to the First Southern group to begin a new era of banking in Lancaster and Central Kentucky. Jess Correll and Randy Attkisson reformed this bank to higher standards and new levels of management. They established the River Foundation for the purpose of giving to Christ-centered organization. This foundation has supported local ministries as well as foreign mission work in places like India and Africa. About ten years ago this foundation helped McKinley Dailey and others to furnish an expensive electric wheel chair to a quadriplegic.

In 1988 my family started building rental property in Nicholasville. Harold Layton was our able loan officer. I recall driving him up to Nicholasville and inspecting some of our first buildings.

Not long after this, in about 1989, a good friend of mine, McKinley Dailey took over our banking business. We not only have benefited from his ability in lending but have used him to coach in the Little League baseball program. Now, my family depends on Mitzi Gilliam and McKinley for all of our banking needs. Many on the board of directors have been good customers of our lumber yard during and after the turn of the century. The Ayres family, the Irvin Group and many others have been excellent customers to our current business.

Lancaster, Kentucky

1st Southern Bank

Citizens Bank Lancaster KY

347

L to R-Hob Bastin, unidentified, Hugh Logan, Elsie Walker, Joe Walker, Sue Shelby Mason, Mom Blakeman, Van Logan, taken in 1951 in front of Mom Blakeman's restaurant with the future library in the background.

Sources

Chapter 1: Deep Are the Roots

The Memoirs of Henley V. Bastin

Chamber of Commerce, Caswell County, North Carolina

The Central Record (weekly 1900-1910)

Memories of conversations with family members

Chapter 2: The Telephone Business

Telephone, the First Hundred Years, John Brooks, Harper & Row, 1975

Memoirs of Henley V. Bastin

The Central Record (weekly 1900-1914)

Telephone History, 1910-1940 www.telephonemuseum.com/History

Chapter3: Luther Herron, the Police Chief

The Harrodsburg Herald (weekly) 1901-1906

The Central Record (weekly) 1905-1927

Garrard County Census, Harold Kurtz, 1920

Murder, Mayhem and Mischief, Jack Bailey

Deposition of Saufley Hughes, November 23, 1920

Conversations with the following: Cecil Arnold, Alvin Brickey, J.W. Marsee, Stacy May, Cecil Sanders, letter of Shirley Hurd (grand niece of Luther Herron), Margaret Simpson

Chapter 4: Our Best Customer Was Shot? James I. Hamilton Duel and Sequel

The Central Record (1900-1924)

Notes of Ben Arnold (unpublished)

Change and Continuity in Twentieth Century America, John Braeman, Ohio State University Press 1968

America in the Twenties, Geoffrey Perrett, Simon and Schuster 1982

The Mind of the South, W.J. Cash, Doubleday and Company, Garden City, New York, 1941

Only Yesterday, Frederick L. Allen, 1931

Conversations with the following: Cecil Arnold, Woodie Leavell, Johnson Price, James Davis, John White, Gordon Bourne, Alvin Brickey, Joan Luxson, Robert and Judith Shearer, Judy Clark, and family members.

Chapter 5: The First Diversification: Henley and Ross 1914-1927

Memoirs of Henley V. Bastin

The Central Record (1914-1924)

Statement of Henley V. Bastin to the city council asking for a rate increase, April 5, 1920

Chapter 6: Bastin Lumber Co. 1914-1921: Alford Bastin Era

Memoirs of Henley V. Bastin

The Central Record (1914-1921)

Chapter 7: Bastin Lumber Co. 1921-1943: Hob Bastin-Bob Goff Era

Bastin Lumber Company Records

The Central Record (1921-1943)

Chapter 8: The Bob Goff Shooting

The Central Record (1920-1937)

Conversations with the following: Cecil Sanders, Caywood Metcalf, Lewis Layton, Alvin Brickey, Cecil Arnold, Hob Bastin, Ross Bastin.

Chapter 9: Bastin Lumber Co. 1943-1965: Ross Bastin Era

The Central Record (1943-1965)

Bastin Lumber Company Records

Chapter 10: Bastin Lumber Co. 1966-Current: Hal Bastin Era

The Central Record (1966-2006)

Bastin Lumber Company Records

Chapter 11: The Education of a Lumber Dealer

Cynthiana High School Yearbook 1955

Chapter 12: Collections

Bastin Lumber Company Records